microwave cooking times

carolyn humphries

updated from the original by jan orchard

foulsham

LONDON • NEW YORK • TORONTO • SYDNEY

foulsham

The Publishing House, Bennetts Close, Cippenham,
Slough, Berkshire, SL1 5AP, England

ISBN 0–572–02750-8

Cover photograph by Peter Howard Smith

Printed in Great Britain by Cox & Wyman, Reading

Contents

Introduction

Your microwave should be your kitchen's greatest asset. Many people use one exclusively; I prefer to use mine in conjunction with my conventional cooker to get the best of both worlds. But whether you are cooking for a large family or living on your own, microwave cooking is fast, convenient and economical. It also reduces the washing up, because many foods that normally stick with a vengeance to the saucepan or dish – boiled milk, scrambled eggs or porridge for example – don't stick at all when cooked in the microwave. In addition, many dishes can be cooked and served in the same container, making things even simpler and quicker.

To get the most out of your microwave, you need to understand how it works and learn a few basic principles, such as what containers you can and can't use and how to adapt your normal cooking methods when necessary. I have set out all this information in the first half of this book. In the second part, I explain exactly how to defrost, cook and reheat every type of food you can successfully prepare in your microwave oven to achieve the best possible results with confidence. This new, improved *Microwave Cooking Times* will be the most useful microwave cookery book you have ever bought, and with it to hand you need never be wary of your microwave oven again.

Understanding Your Microwave Oven

What is microwaving?

In a conventional cooker, heat is radiated round the food, cooking it from the outside inwards. This gives it the traditional brown, cooked appearance on the surface. In a microwave cooker, the food is cooked by microwaves, which are similar to radio waves. They are converted from ordinary electricity using a magnetron, situated in the top of the microwave oven. The microwaves penetrate the food to a depth of about 5 cm/2 in and cause the water molecules in the food to vibrate. This in turn produces friction, creating heat, which cooks the food. Because there is no external heat source, the food does not brown or crisp on the surface. This can be achieved, however, by various methods that I shall suggest on pages 22–5.

The power output of different models of microwave varies, and this will make a considerable difference to how long foods take to cook. A low-wattage oven (600 watts) will take longer than a 700 watt oven, which, in turn, will take longer than an 800 watt oven. The ovens with an output of 900–1000 watts are, of course, faster still, but I find that for the best results it is sometimes better to cook foods on 70 per cent power (Medium-High) instead of Full Power in these very high wattage ovens. I shall explain more about this in the section on Power Output Settings (see pages 7–10).

Foods react to microwaves instantly, so they cook very quickly. They also continue to cook after you turn off the cooker, because the molecules continue to vibrate, only gradually slowing down until they stop. The vibration – and cooking – goes on even if you take the food out of the oven. This is why it is important to take the 'standing time' into account as food will carry on cooking during that time. It also means that you should never completely cook food when microwaving, but remove it when it is still slightly underdone. It will be cooked to perfection after the designated standing time. If you do miscalculate and it is still slightly undercooked, you can pop it back in for a few more seconds.

Different types of microwave oven

Most of you will already have a microwave in the kitchen, but if you are buying for the first time, or replacing your old machine, there are a few things for you to consider when making your choice.

Microwaves come in several different types. There are the inexpensive, basic models that simply provide defrosting and cooking facilities; some may have variable heat settings. These are perfectly adequate if you only want to defrost and reheat ready meals and rarely want to cook items from scratch. Their main drawback is that the capacity of the oven tends to be small, which will limit the quantity you can cook.

Next are the models with variable heat settings, auto-defrost and auto-cook facilities. These tend to be larger than the basic models and are best for straightforward microwave cooking.

The third option is a microwave with auto-defrost and auto-cook settings plus a built-in grill (broiler) or browning element. These give you the added option of being able to brown your food after cooking, or to use the grill on its own for such foods as thin pieces of meat or fish, burgers, toasted sandwiches, cheese on toast, etc. The grill operates with the door shut and the turntable, if there is one, rotates to give even browning. The grill is usually preheated before use. This is my preferred type of microwave oven.

The final option is a combination cooker. These machines use a combination of hot air (to brown and crisp the surface) and microwaves, thus reducing normal cooking times by about half. Some cookers use the radiant heat of a grill element to heat the air, while others have an element that heats up behind the back wall of the cooker. The air is circulated by a fan and the results are extremely good, particularly for cakes, gratin dishes, crumbles and roasted vegetables and meats. Bread and scones (biscuits), too, rise beautifully. The only disadvantage is that you don't get as much of the delicious smell of baking you do with a conventional cooker (this, of course, is turned into a bonus when you are cooking strong-smelling fish or veggie dishes!). These machines can replace a conventional cooker, but as the oven capacity is very limited, you have to cook one dish at a time instead of putting everything in together as you would in a conventional oven. This wipes out any fuel-saving and may prove to be more labour-intensive. But it is a good choice if you are cooking for one or two people at the most.

Power output settings

Different microwave ovens also have different power output settings. There is no standard power indicator on them, so it's important to know the percentage output of each setting. For instance, when using 100 per cent output, some microwaves call this Full Power (as I have in this book), others call it High and others have the actual maximum wattage output (e.g. 1000 watts) on the dial or programmer. To make it even more complicated, I have recently come across one cooker that uses High for 70 per cent power and Full Power for 100 per cent! This chart shows the right settings, based on a 1000 watt cooker, but remember, it is the percentage of power used that is important.

Percentage	Description	Number on dial	Wattage
10%	Low/Warm	1	100w
30%	Medium-Low/Defrost	2	300w
50%	Medium/Simmer	3	500w
70%	Medium-High/Roast	4	700w
100%	High/Full Power	5	1000w

Using the settings

There are five different power levels on most ovens. Many foods are best when cooked on 100 per cent (which I refer to as Full Power). But if you have a high wattage oven, you may get better results cooking on 70 per cent (Medium-High) because the microwaves are so fierce. Check your manufacturer's instructions, and try both ways to see which results are best. In all cookers, some foods benefit from more gentle cooking. The table overleaf gives you a guide:

Full Power (100%)	Medium-High (70%)	Medium (50%)	Medium-Low (30%)	Low (10%)
For quick cooking of rashers (slices) of bacon, tender poultry, meat steaks, fish, fruit, vegetables, bread, cakes and puddings. Reheating leftovers. Heating a browning dish (see page 23).	Cakes and puddings. Roasting meat and poultry. Cooking and reheating bread. Especially useful with high-wattage cookers.	Simmering stews and casseroles, soups, eggs, cream and cheese dishes. Reheating frozen meals.	Defrosting. Slow-cooking curries and casseroles. Cooking custards. Softening butter and ripening cheese.	Keeping foods warm. Infusing milk and sauces for flavour. Very gentle defrosting.

Labelling

* Reproduced courtesy of the Department for Environment, Food and Rural Affairs.

Most new domestic microwave ovens now display a label that ties in with the labels on food packs, referring to microwave cooking. Simply match the information on the food pack with that on the oven to give the heating time needed. The oven label, an example of which is given below, shows three important pieces of information.

the microwave symbol →

→ the power output (watts)

← the heating category for small packs

The microwave symbol
The microwave symbol shows that the oven has been labelled in compliance with the new scheme.

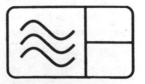

The power output

The figure in this box shows the power output of the oven, in watts, based on an internationally agreed standard (IEC 705).

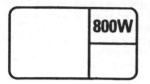

If your oven is rated 700 watt, it will heat food faster than a 600 watt oven, but not as fast as a 800/850 watt or 900/1000 watt oven, as shown below.

oven power rating

| 500W | 600W | 700W | 800W |

◀ more heating time   less heating time ▶

The heating category

In this box, there will be a letter. This is the heating category based on your oven's ability to heat small food packs.

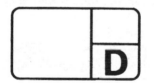

Instructions on food packs weighing up to 500 g (18 oz) are likely to be given in terms of these letters.

If your oven is category C, it will heat up small portions of food faster than category A or B but not as fast as a category D or E oven, as shown below.

heating category for small packs

| A | B | C | D | E |

◀ more heating time   less heating time ▶

〰 T O   M I C R O W A V E

For ovens marked with a heating category, select appropriate time(s) for your oven. For other ovens, refer to timings given for oven wattage. When using ovens of different power, heating time must be increased or decreased accordingly. Always check that the food is piping hot before serving.

heating category		oven wattage	
B	D	650W	750W
6	5	5	4
m i n u t e s		m i n u t e s	

The food pack label
Most packaged food suitable for microwaving will be marked with the microwave symbol and appropriate instructions for heating. Below is an illustration of the type of label used.

Using heating category instructions
In the illustration above, information is given for B and D ovens only. You can adjust this to suit your own oven, if different.

For C ovens, choose the time midway between B and D, in this case 5½ minutes.

For A ovens, it will be necessary to heat food for a little longer than the time given for B ovens, in this case 6½ minutes.

For E ovens, use a slightly shorter heating time than that specified for D ovens, in this case 4½ minutes.

Using oven wattage instructions
In the illustration on pages 8–9, information is given for 650 watt and 750 watt ovens. Again, these can be adjusted to suit your oven if it is different.

For ovens with a wattage lower than 650 watts, heat for a longer time. In this example, a 500 watt oven will need approximately 6 minutes. A 600 watt oven will be similar to a 650 watt oven but may need a little longer.

For ovens with wattage higher than 750 watts, heat for a slightly shorter time. In this case, an 800–850 watt oven will need approximately 3 minutes and a 900–1000 watt cooker will need about 2½ minutes.

After heating, always check food is piping hot throughout. If not, heat for a little longer.

Foodline

If you need further help to understand the instructions on food packs, a free helpline is available through the Food Safety Advisory Centre to offer practical advice. Call freephone 020 7808 7256.

Containers and equipment

It is important that you use suitable containers and equipment when cooking in the microwave, in order to ensure not only best results but also your safety and the long life of your oven. There is a huge range of containers and equipment now available for use with microwaves. Not all of it is necessary, however. In many cases, you can use your ordinary kitchenware.

You will find that you use fewer dishes when microwave cooking, because many of the dishes you would normally use just for serving food can also be used for the cooking. You must make sure that whatever dishes you use are microwave-safe, however.

You can use: Ovenproof glass dishes, glazed earthenware, dishwasher-safe porcelain, pottery and boilable plastic; also basketware and wood for very short times only, like warming bread rolls.

You can't use: Metal bakeware, ironstone, thin plastics or any crockery with metal trim.

The dish test: To test if a container is suitable for microwave cooking, stand half a cup of water in the dish to be tested. Microwave on Full Power for 1 minute. If the dish feels cool but the water is hot, it is fine to use. If the dish feels hot and the water is cool, the dish absorbs microwaves and should not be used.

Shape and size

The size and shape of a container is very important when cooking in the microwave. Round, oval or rectangular dishes with rounded corners give the best results, because the microwaves are distributed more evenly. If the dish is too small, the food could bubble over and it will take longer to cook as it is so densely packed. If the dish is too big, the food may become dry and overcook. Shallow dishes of food will cook more quickly than deep ones. For best results, remember the following general rules.

- Choose straight-sided containers and, if a lid is going to be needed, a casserole dish (Dutch oven) is ideal.

- For vegetables etc., choose a dish large enough to hold them in a single layer.

- For a recipe cooked in liquid, such as a casserole, make sure there is about 5 cm/2 in of space above all the ingredients to allow enough room for it to boil.

- For cakes and bread, use a dish with enough height to allow for rising.

Utensils

Metal utensils, such as spoons or whisks, can be used to stir food but should never be left in the microwave during cooking. A spoon rest at the side of the cooker is a good idea to avoid mess on your worktop.

Wooden spoons can be left in foods that need repeated stirring during microwaving, but only for short periods of time. However, make sure the spoon does not touch the top or sides of the oven during microwaving.

Microwave racks

These are specially coated racks with feet. They are placed in the oven to lift foods off the floor, thus allowing air and microwaves to circulate more freely. They can also be used when you want juices or other liquids to drain away from the food being cooked.

Microwave domes or lids

These are very useful for covering plated meals or any foods that require reheating. You can, of course, use an inverted dinner plate or a cereal bowl instead, or the lid of a casserole dish (Dutch oven).

Microwave stacking rings

If you want to microwave several plated meals at one time, the easiest way is by using stacking rings. These allow you to stack up to four plates on top of each other with air circulating between them. You must rearrange the plates during heating, however, so that they all receive the same amount of energy.

Microwave meat thermometers and probes

Microwave thermometers are specially designed to be inserted in the meat or poultry and can be used while the microwave is on. (A conventional meat thermometer can only inserted once the meat is removed from the microwave.) Some microwaves have a probe, which is attached to the inside of the oven. It is inserted into the meat and the cooker will switch off automatically when the meat reaches the correct temperature. This may be lower than you expect, but remember that the temperature of the meat will continue to rise on standing as it completes cooking.

The meat should always feel tender when tested with a skewer and the juices should run clear when poultry is pierced in the thickest part of the thigh with a skewer, but the temperature is a more accurate indicator when checking the joint or bird is cooked.

Browning dishes

A browning dish is a specially designed microwave dish that absorbs microwave energy and so browns the surface of foods cooked on it. It can be used to sear and cook meat, poultry, sausages, eggs, and even pizzas and toasted sandwiches. For more information on how to use browning dishes, see pages 22–3.

The Principles of Microwave Cooking

Microwaving is not an exact science. The quality, thickness, size and shape of the foods – and of the container they are in – all make a difference to how long they require to cook. In this book I give approximate cooking times but in general it is always wisest to undercook rather than overcook. You can always test and cook for a little longer if necessary. As you become more experienced, you will learn to tell quickly how long foods will take and how to cook them to perfection. Microwave cooking is no more difficult than cooking in a conventional oven, but it is different.

General principles

- Unlike a conventional oven, the amount of food you put in a microwave will affect the cooking time. So the more items you put into your microwave to be cooked, the more the cooking time must be increased. This is because the number of microwaves is always the same, so if they have to be distributed through more food there will be less energy per item. So, where one jacket potato will take about 4 minutes, two will take 7–8 minutes, depending on the output of your cooker.

- Dense foods take longer to cook. For instance, a jacket potato will take around 4 minutes, but a baked apple will take less than half that time. Also a prepared dish that cannot be stirred will take longer than one which can be rearranged during cooking, as the heat cannot be redistributed during the cooking process.

- Thicker parts of foods should be placed towards the outside of the dish. For example, arrange chicken drumsticks with the bony ends pointing towards the centre of the dish. When cooking vegetables such as broccoli, the florets should be arranged with the stalks outwards.

- Foods at room temperature will cook more quickly than those straight from the fridge or freezer.

- Foods with a high fat or sugar content will get very hot quickly. They can burn, so cook carefully and do not use plastic containers as they may melt. Always handle with oven gloves or you could burn your hands.

- It is not usually necessary to grease dishes when cooking in the microwave unless you are using a browning dish. If greasing is recommended, as in the case of some puddings, brush very sparingly with oil or melted butter or margarine. Too much fat will impair the finished dish.

- Most foods will not crisp and brown but meat or poultry with a high fat content will colour naturally after about 10 minutes. Bacon rashers (slices) and pork crackling will crisp on standing.

- Pastry (paste) will burn if overcooked and so will foods with a high sugar content, like chocolate. Bread, on the other hand, goes wonderfully soft when reheated but will become rubbery or completely hard if overheated. Seconds can be crucial.

Stirring and turning

Many microwaves have a built-in turntable to turn the food while cooking to help distribute the microwaves more evenly. Alternatively, your oven may have paddles or stirrers concealed in either the base or the top of the oven to do a similar job.

It is important to stir and turn food during cooking too. If you don't, you will have hot or cold spots in your food where the microwaves have been concentrated or have not reached. It is vital that food is piping hot and cooked thoroughly before it is served. All recipes tell you when to do this. Also, remember always to stir reheated drinks before sipping. The surface of the liquid will be scalding, even if it is cooler underneath. Once stirred, your drink will be evenly hot.

Timing

Timing is all-important when cooking with a microwave. As I have said, the length of time a food takes to cook depends on its size, shape and density, the amount of fat and sugar it contains and even the size and shape of the dish it is cooked in.

Cooking times also vary from one microwave to another, depending on the output of the oven. In this book, the times are given as a guide to the range of outputs from the lowest (600 watt) to the highest (900–1000 watt). When microwave ovens were first introduced, they were often as low as 500 watt. These are not common now, however, so I have not included them. If you do have a low-output cooker such as this, add on an extra 20 seconds per minute to the **longest** cooking times given in this book.

As a general guide, the higher the power output, the more quickly it will cook. I have categorised ovens as 600–650 watt, 700–750 watt, 800–850 watt and 900–1000 watt. Even within these categories there may be some variation, but don't worry. The times in this book are minimum times, and you can always add on a little extra if necessary.

Always cook for the shortest time given, check and cook a little longer if necessary. The more you use your microwave, the more you will get used to how long particular tasks take in your model and can then cook more confidently for specific times. Do note that the recipes in some microwave cookery books may have been tested using only one level of output – older books may use 600 watts, and newer ones 750 or 850 watts. The very latest may use 900–1000 watts.

The high wattage cookers (800–1000 watts) are so fast that the cooking times differ by literally only a few seconds per minute, but those few seconds are vital. So if you have one of these, cook for the shorter time, check and add on a few seconds if necessary.

If your oven has a different wattage to those used in a microwave recipe book, you can alter the cooking times as follows:

If the recipe is written for 700 watts and your oven is 600 watts – increase cooking time by up to 20 seconds per minute.

If the recipe is written for 700 watts and your oven is 800 watts – decrease cooking time by up to 20 seconds per minute.

If the recipe is for 800 watts and your oven is 1000 watts – decrease cooking time by 10 seconds per minute, 'rounding up' to the nearest 5 seconds. Test and add on a little, if necessary.

The cooking times when using Medium-Low or Low settings vary very little whatever the power output.

If you have a 900–1000 watt cooker, you may find you get better results for some foods by cooking on Medium-High for slightly longer than on Full Power. Trial and error is the only way.

Adjusting quantities

If you want to cook a larger or smaller quantity of food than stated in a microwave recipe, follow these general rules.

Increasing the quantities
- Use a larger dish.

- If you increase the quantity of food by a half, increase the cooking time by about a third. If you double the quantity, increase the cooking time by a half. For example, if the recipe is for four people and takes 12 minutes, allow 16 minutes for six people. If you are making enough to serve eight, cook for about 18 minutes.

- Calculate the increased standing time in the same way.

- Cook for less time than you calculated, test, then add on extra time in short bursts, testing as you go.

- Remember that you should not try to cook huge amounts of food in your microwave all at once. The microwaves need to penetrate as much of the food as possible, so there must be room to stir or rearrange it. Large single items do not cook successfully. A very thick joint, for instance, is likely to overcook on the outside before the centre is cooked, even if you turn it over during cooking, as the same part of the food is being continually blasted. You can overcome this to some extent by removing the joint for standing time, halfway through cooking.

- Remember, the bigger the quantity, the longer it takes. So if, for instance, you wanted to bake 12 large potatoes and a large casserole for a party, it would make more sense to cook everything altogether in your conventional cooker, than try to cook it all in the microwave!

Reducing the quantities
• Use a smaller dish.

• If cooking half the quantity, reduce the cooking time by about a third. If cooking a quarter of the quantity, reduce the cooking time by about two-thirds. For example, if a recipe serves four people and takes 12 minutes to cook, the quantity for two people will take about 8 minutes, and the quantity for one will take about 4 minutes.

• Calculate the reduction in standing time in the same way.

• As always, cook for a little less time than you calculate, test, then add on more time in short bursts, continuing to test as you go. Once you know the timings of a particular recipe, note them down for future reference.

• If cooking very small amounts of food – like a small amount of chocolate or one wedge of pizza – put a cup of water in the microwave beside the food. It will absorb some of the energy, preventing the food from overheating too quickly.

Covering foods

As a guide, foods which need to be covered when cooking conventionally need to be covered when microwaving. For best results, follow these general rules.

• Cover foods that may splutter with a dome of greaseproof (waxed) paper or a piece of kitchen paper (paper towel).

• Clingfilm (plastic wrap) is ideal for covering dishes where you want to keep moisture in. Pierce it in several places or roll back one corner to allow steam to escape otherwise it will billow up during cooking. Also make sure it does not touch the food during cooking. A dish with a lid is a good alternative.

Note: It is not recommended that you use ordinary clingfilm in the microwave. It has been found that the diezethylhexedipate

(DEHA) used in the manufacture to make it stretchy can pass into food during cooking although it is not known to what degree this may be harmful. Make sure that any clingfilm you use is suitable for use in the microwave. It will be stated clearly on the packaging. If there are no instructions for use in the microwave, do not use it.

- When cooking dishes containing liquids, use a microwave cover or a casserole dish (Dutch oven) with a lid. Alternatively, a plate that fits over the container is just as good.

- Microwave plates with lids and microwave domes are good for reheating plated meals. Alternatively, put the food on an ordinary microwave-safe dinner plate and invert another plate, bowl or a casserole dish lid to cover the food to prevent drying around the edges during heating.

- Don't cover cakes or breads when cooking.

- Roaster bags can be used in a microwave. They are good for poultry and joints. They help to brown the food as well as preventing spluttering and they keep the food moist. Don't use any metal ties provided with them, however. Tie with plastic ties, string or elastic bands. If you are roasting a joint and you don't want it to 'stew' in the bag, place the bag containing the joint in a casserole dish and pierce the bottom of the bag so the excess juices drain into the dish. Alternatively, put the joint in the pierced bag on a microwave rack or upturned plate over a large plate to catch the juices. If there's room, you can put both the joint and the microwave rack or upturned plate inside the bag, but don't pierce the bottom of the bag.

- Non-stick baking parchment is suitable for freezing as well as microwaving so is good for lining dishes or covering food that is to be cooked, then frozen, or vice versa.

Shielding and arcing
Generally you should not use foil for microwave cooking as it is metallic. But you can use small smooth strips to shield wing tips, bone ends or thin parts of food that would otherwise overcook or dry out. This is called shielding. If you use too much or it is too

crumpled, arcing will occur, which can damage the oven. You can use foil, shiny-side in, to cover cooked food when taken out of the microwave for its standing time before serving. It is ideal, for instance, to wrap individual, cooked, jacket potatoes. They will then finish cooking and keep hot for up to an hour. It is also useful for covering partly defrosted foods, such as a joint of meat, while it finishes defrosting at room temperature (see Defrosting, below).

Recipe conversion

Most conventional recipes can be cooked in the microwave. You will need to alter them a little, however, and it will be necessary to experiment to get the best from your machine. I've given tips throughout the book for specific dishes. For best results, follow these general rules for conversion.

- When cooking soups and casseroles, use only two-thirds the amount of liquid stated in the conventional recipe.

- Cut the conventional cooking time by three-quarters if cooking on Full Power.

- Cut the conventional cooking time by half if cooking on Medium.

- Cut the conventional cooking time by a quarter if cooking on Medium-Low.

- Cover a dish in the microwave if you would cover it in the conventional oven.

- Remember that food will continue cooking during standing time, so don't overcook.

Defrosting

Many microwaves now have automatic defrost facility. Simply follow the manufacturer's instructions on selecting the item to be defrosted. Tap in its weight, start the oven and it will pulse energy on and off until defrosting is complete and tell you when to turn the food. Standing time is built in. It is impossible to be absolutely precise about exact defrosting times, however, as so many factors may affect it, so it is important to check occasionally to ensure that the item does not start to cook. Some items are best only partially defrosted in the microwave and then left to complete defrosting at room temperature.

For best results, follow these general principles.

- Defrosting is usually carried out at Medium-Low (30 per cent power) but if you have a 900–1000 watt oven you may find it best to use Low (10 per cent power). Unlike cooking on Full Power, the timing varies very little whatever the output of your model.

- The rules for arranging foods and their size and shape (see pages 14–15) apply to defrosting as well as cooking.

- If defrosting meat or other foods where you don't want to use the liquid that drips out, place on a microwave rack with a container underneath so the liquid will drip away from the food.

- Defrost in short bursts only, with standing time in between. If you microwave for too long, you'll start to cook the outside.

- Check food before the end of the given defrosting time and remember it will continue to defrost during standing.

- When defrosting minced (ground) meat, scrape off the meat as it defrosts and remove from the oven. Freeflow mince can be cooked from frozen.

- Break up casseroles, soups or other foods frozen in a block as soon as possible and move the frozen pieces to the edge.

- Ease apart pieces of food such as chops, diced meat, sliced bread and bacon rashers (slices) as they defrost to allow more even distribution of the microwaves.

- If defrosting food in a bag, flex the bag occasionally to distribute the microwaves evenly.

- Small items of meat and poultry, such as chops, steaks and poultry pieces, can be defrosted completely in the microwave but you should not try to defrost large joints or whole poultry completely. Start the process, then leave at room temperature, wrapped in foil, shiny side in, to finish defrosting. Salmonella, a nasty form of food poisoning, can occur if the flesh starts to cook before it is completely defrosted.

- Protect bone ends and thin ends of meat, poultry or fish with small strips of smooth foil as they defrost, to protect them from beginning to cook while the rest of the food completes defrosting. Don't use large pieces or arcing will occur.

- Put cakes, bread and desserts on a piece of kitchen paper (paper towel) to absorb moisture as they defrost.

- Don't try to defrost cream desserts, such as cheesecakes, completely. Start the process in the microwave, then let them completely defrost at room temperature.

- Remove any metal containers, twist ties or lids before defrosting in the microwave.

- Vegetables can be cooked straight from frozen. Bags of frozen peas, for instance, can be cooked in their bag.

You will find specific times for defrosting different foods in the second half of the book.

Reheating

Many foods can be reheated successfully in the microwave and this is one of the most commonly used functions of microwave ovens. It is important to turn or stir foods as appropriate to distribute the heat and to make sure that they are piping hot before serving, never just warm or even fairly hot. See the individual entries in the main chapters for specific instructions.

Browning

Browning does not happen naturally in the microwave, but there are various ways to achieve a similar result.

Browning dishes
These provide the best and simplest way to brown foods in the microwave. Always follow the manufacturer's instructions. Wear oven gloves when handling a browning dish after heating and don't place it directly on your work surface as it gets extremely hot.

Preheat the dish for 4–8 minutes, according to your microwave output. Add a knob of butter or margarine or 15 ml/1 tbsp oil and swirl round to cover the whole surface. Add the food to be cooked, pressing it down on the plate, thinnest parts towards the centre. Cook on Full Power according to the table below.

Type of food	Preparation	Quantity	Cooking time
Chips (fries)	Spread in an even layer	2 portions	3–6 minutes, turning once
Chops	Sprinkle with dried herbs and/or pepper, if liked	2 large or 4 small	4–6 minutes, turning once
Fish fingers	Cook from frozen	4 fingers	2–3 minutes, turning once
Fish cakes	Cook from frozen	4 cakes	4–6 minutes, turning once
Fried eggs	Prick the yolks with a cocktail stick (toothpick)	4 eggs	3–4 minutes, on Medium
Gammon/ bacon steaks	Snip the edges with scissors to prevent curling	2 medium	3–5 minutes, turning once
Hamburgers	Don't grease the dish	4 small or 2 quarter-pounders	2–4 minutes, turning once
Liver	Cut into thin slices and season with pepper	8 thin slices	2–3 minutes, turning once
Potato waffles	Cook from frozen	2 large or 4 small	3–4 minutes, turning once
Pizza	Cook from frozen	1 small	4–6 minutes
Sausages	Prick with a fork and don't grease the dish	8 chipolatas 8 large	2–4 minutes 4–6 minutes turning once
Steaks	Sprinkle with steak seasoning, pepper or dried herbs	2 × 225 g/ 8 oz	4–8 minutes turning once
Toasted sandwiches	Butter the bread on the outside and don't grease the dish	2 rounds	2–3 minutes, turning once

Reheat the dish for half the original time if cooking a second batch of food.

Other ways of browning foods

Browning can also be achieved by adding ingredients before, during or after cooking. These can give both colour and extra texture.

Before cooking:
- Brush meat and poultry with:
  Melted butter or oil and dust with paprika
  or
  Mushroom or tomato ketchup (catsup), or Worcestershire, soy, brown or barbecue sauce, mixed with an equal quantity of water
  or
  Warm honey, mixed with a good dash of soy sauce and a good squeeze of lemon juice.

- Quickly sear and brown the surfaces of meat or poultry in a frying pan (skillet).

- Dip chops, steaks or poultry portions in beaten egg, then dried or toasted breadcrumbs, toasted nuts or sesame seeds, crushed crisps (potato chips), corn or branflakes or stuffing mix.

- Marinate meat or poultry in a marinade containing soy sauce, tomato or red wine to impart a good rich colour to the flesh.

Halfway through cooking:
- Brush with a sticky glaze such as:
  Redcurrant jelly (clear conserve)
  or
  Shredless marmalade
  or
  A mixture of clear honey and wholegrain or Dijon mustard.

After cooking:
- Place the cooked dish under a preheated grill (broiler) for a few minutes, to brown any toppings and crisp any skin.

Browning cakes and breads

Plain cakes and breads look particularly pallid and uninteresting when cooking in the microwave, but there are several ways of brightening them up. Choose from any of the following.

While making up the mixture:
* Use wholemeal flour rather than white (you may need a little extra liquid) and/or brown sugar instead of white (chocolate and coffee cakes look fine anyway).

* Substitute 15 g/½ oz/2 tbsp custard powder for white flour to improve the colour.

Before cooking:
* Sprinkle the surface of cakes with ground cinnamon, chopped nuts, desiccated (shredded) coconut or chopped glacé (candied) fruits.

* Brush breads or rolls with egg yolk and sprinkle with bulghar (cracked wheat), toasted sesame seeds or poppy seeds.

* Brush scones (biscuits) with melted butter or margarine and sprinkle with toasted sesame seeds or chopped nuts or demerara sugar (for sweet ones).

Halfway through cooking:
* Sprinkle cakes and sweet scones with a mixture of demerara or light or dark brown sugar and chopped, toasted nuts.

After cooking:
* Dust with sifted icing (confectioners') sugar or coat in butter cream, icing (frosting) or melted chocolate.

Maintenance and Troubleshooting

Cleaning

To get the best out of your microwave and ensure its long life, you should spend a little time cleaning it regularly. Fortunately, this is a simple matter, since food splashes do not burn on in the way they do in a conventional oven.

• Always wipe up any spills straight away or they will attract the microwaves next time you cook, which could affect the cooking time. Microwaves can't differentiate between food to be cooked and crumbs, mucky dribbles or splatters.

• Wipe out the inside with a dry cloth or kitchen paper (paper towels) after use to remove any condensation that may cause rust in time.

• Make sure door seals are kept clean or microwaves could escape.

• To freshen the interior (after cooking fish, for instance), put 300 ml/½ pt/1¼ cups water, a few slices of lemon and a clean cloth into a bowl. Heat on Full Power for 3–5 minutes until boiling. Leave until lukewarm, then squeeze out the cloth and wipe all over the surfaces of the interior. Dry with a dry cloth or kitchen paper (paper towels).

• Never use scourers or oven cleaners on your machine.

Follow the manufacturer's instructions for cleaning a combination oven.

Troubleshooting

If you think your oven is not working properly, there are several simple checks you can do before calling out an engineer.

• Check the oven is properly plugged in.

- Check the wires in the flex have not worked loose from the plug pins.

- Check the fuse has not blown.

- Check the oven door is shut properly.

- Check the oven is not set to 'hold', 'timer' or 'auto'.

- Make sure the air vent is clear and there is nothing heavy on top of the oven.

Do's and don'ts for your microwave

- Do read your manufacturer's instruction booklet properly.

- Do make sure your oven is plugged in using a properly earthed, fused plug in a normal 13 amp socket.

- Do make sure the oven has an airspace of at least 10 cm/4 in behind it to allow air to circulate freely.

- Do use your normal household kitchenware for cooking and serving food but make sure it is microwave-safe first. If you are unsure, perform the dish test (see page 11).

- Don't use metal containers or utensils in the microwave or large pieces of foil or metal ties.

- Don't use sealed containers as these could burst with the build-up of steam.

- Don't try to deep-fry foods in your oven – the oil temperature cannot be controlled.

- Don't turn on the oven when empty. Keep a cup of water in it when not in use to prevent this.

- Don't put cans of food in the microwave.

- Don't use the cooker if it is damaged in any way – especially if the door is loose or if the seals are faulty.

- Don't try and repair a microwave oven yourself. If the quick troubleshooting checks given above don't work, call out an approved service engineer.

Convenience Foods

Microwaves and convenience foods make a perfect partnership. You can often defrost, reheat and serve a dish in the same container, which saves time and washing up. I can't stress enough, though, that you must make sure food is **piping hot** throughout before serving – not just nicely warm – otherwise germs can breed and serious food poisoning can result.

In this section, you'll find general hints and defrosting and heating times for many favourite convenience foods. If I refer to a frozen item (such as a frozen lasagne) and you have a cooked and chilled one, simply omit the defrosting time and use only the reheating time. If you have taken your dish straight from the fridge, however, you may need to add a little extra heating time.

The 'piping hot' test

Food must be piping hot throughout, not just warm. The best test is to insert a knife down through the centre of the heated food. Hold there for 5 seconds, then remove. The blade should be burning hot to touch. If not, microwave a little longer and check again.

Reheating ready-made foods

Many ready-made foods can be reheated in the microwave, for example, pizzas, baked beans, canned pasta, soups and stews, frozen and cook-chill meals. Follow the manufacturer's instructions on the packet or can. Always remove any foil containers and empty canned foods into a bowl. Stir canned foods and cook-chill items in sauces several times during heating to distribute the heat evenly. Remember always to pierce the bag of boil-in-the-bag foods.

Plated meals

Always arrange plated meals with the densest, thickest foods towards the outside of the plate. Ideally, leave the centre clear or containing only peas or other low-density items. Potatoes, in particular, take quite a while to reheat. Make sure they are not cut too large. Also, make sure the food is completely covered with a lid or dome before reheating or the edges are likely to dry out before the centre is heated. It is a good idea to add gravy or a sauce too, to prevent drying.

To test whether the food is hot throughout, touch the centre of the underside of the plate with your fingers. It should feel piping hot.

You can heat several plated meals at the same time, using microwave stacking rings (see page 12). Rearrange the plates during heating so that they all receive the same amount of microwave energy.

Pies

You can't cook these successfully in the microwave but they can be reheated (see individual entries). Take care not to overheat or the pastry (paste) will be unpalatably tough. You can, if necessary, crisp the crust under a hot grill (broiler) after heating, but take care not to burn it!

Defrosting and heating times for convenience foods

Frozen ready-meals can be cooked from frozen on Medium, but for best results defrost, then cook. As a rough guide to the time for cooking from frozen on Medium, add together the defrost and cooking times given on the following pages.

Canned baked beans or pasta

Reheating: Empty the beans into a bowl or serving dish.
Stir once or twice during heating.

Quantity	Time on Full Power			
	600–650w	700–750w	800–850w	900–1000w
425 g/15 oz/ 1 large can	4 mins	3 mins	3 mins	2½–3 mins
225 g/8 oz/ 1 small can	2 mins	1½ mins	1 min	1 min

Standing time: None.

Stir and serve.

Canned baked beans or pasta on toast

Reheating: Make the toast in the normal way and butter, if liked. Place on a serving plate. Spoon 1 quantity of cold baked beans over.

Quantity	Time on Full Power			
	600–650w	700–750w	800–850w	900–1000w
1 portion on toast	2 mins	1½ mins	1 min	1 min

Standing time: None.

Serve straight away.

Canned savoury mince or stew

Reheating: Turn into a dish. Cover with a lid or clingfilm (plastic wrap), rolled back at one edge.

Quantity	Time on Full Power			
	600–650w	700–750w	800–850w	900–1000w
425 g/15 oz/ 1 large can	4–5 mins	3½–4 mins	3–3½ mins	3 mins

For a quick shepherd's pie, after heating, top with mashed potato and flash under a hot grill (broiler) to brown.

Standing time: 2 minutes, covered with a dome of foil.

Canned steak and kidney pudding

Preparation: Remove the pudding from the can and turn out on to a plate. Cover with a pudding basin, large enough not to come in contact with the pudding.

Quantity	Time on Full Power			
	600–650w	700–750w	800–850w	900–1000w
Family-size	7½–9 mins	6–7½ mins	4½–6 mins	4½ mins
Individual	2½–3 mins	2–2½ mins	1½–2 mins	1½ mins

Standing time: 2–3 minutes.

Canned frankfurters

Preparation: Empty with their liquid into a casserole dish (Dutch oven). Shake the dish once or twice during heating.

Quantity	Time on Full Power			
	600–650w	700–750w	800–850w	900–1000w
8–10	3–4 mins	2½–3½ mins	2–3 mins	2½ mins

Standing time: 1 minute.

Drain and serve.

Hot dogs

Preparation: Prick 4 hot dog sausages and place in finger rolls. Wrap individually in kitchen paper (paper towels) and arrange in a circle on a plate or the turntable. If serving with onions, cook these first (see page 138).

Quantity	Time on Full Power			
	600–650w	700–750w	800–850w	900–1000w
4	3 mins	2 mins	1 min	1 min

Standing time: None.

Open the kitchen paper, add cooked onions, if liked, ketchup (catsup) and mustard and serve straight away.

Smoked pork ring

Preparation: Place in its package in a shallow dish. Pierce the bag in several places. Turn over halfway through heating.

Quantity	Time on Full Power			
	600–650w	700–750w	800–850w	900–1000w
1	4 mins	3½ mins	3 mins	2½–3 mins

Standing time: 2 minutes.

Cut open the bag, remove and slice.

Boil-in-the-bag frozen fish in sauce, frozen stew or casserole

Reheat from frozen.

Reheating: Pierce the bag and stand it on a plate.
Flex the bag once or twice during heating.

Alternatively, cook on Medium for an extra ½ – 1 minute.

Quantity	Time on Full Power			
	600–650w	700–750w	800–850w	900–1000w
1 portion	4 mins	3½ mins	3 mins	2½–3 mins

Standing time: 2 minutes.

Frozen macaroni cheese

Defrosting: Remove any foil packaging and place
on a plate or in a dish.

Quantity	Time on Medium-Low (all power outputs)
Family-size	8 mins
Individual	5 mins

Standing time: Family-size: 6 minutes. Individual portion: 2 minutes.

Reheating: Increase the microwave output to Full Power.

Quantity	Time on Full Power			
	600–650w	700–750w	800–850w	900–1000w
Family-size	6 mins	5 mins	4 mins	3½–4 mins
Individual	2 mins	1½ mins	1–1½ mins	1 min

Standing time: 2–3 minutes.

Test with a knife (see page 28) to check it is piping hot.

Frozen plated meal

Defrosting: Remove any foil wrapping.
Cover with a lid or microwave dome.

Quantity	Time on Medium-Low (all power outputs)
1 plate	5 mins

Standing time: 2 minutes.

Reheating: Increase the microwave output to Full Power.

Quantity	Time on Full Power			
	600–650w	700–750w	800–850w	900–1000w
1 plate	4–5 mins	3½–4½ mins	3–4 mins	3–3½ mins

Standing time: 2 minutes.

Yorkshire puddings

Reheating: Put 4–6 puddings in a circle on a sheet of kitchen paper (paper towel) on a plate.

Quantity	Time on Full Power			
	600–650w	700–750w	800–850w	900–1000w
4 large individual or 6 small individual	40 secs	30 secs	20 secs	20 secs

Standing time: 1 minute.

If reheating from frozen, add on a few extra seconds per pudding.

Quiches, flans (pies) and tarts

Defrosting: Remove any foil packaging
and place on a plate or in a flan dish (pie pan).

Quantity	Time on Medium-Low (all power outputs)
1 × 20 cm/8 in	4 mins

Standing time: 5 minutes.

Reheating: Turn the microwave output to Full Power.

Quantity	Time on Full Power			
	600–650w	700–750w	800–850w	900–1000w
1 × 20 cm/8 in	4 mins	3½ mins	3 mins	2½–3 mins

After heating, the pastry (paste) should feel warm and the
filling piping hot. If not, heat for slightly longer.

Standing time: 2 minutes.

Double crust pie

Defrosting: Remove from any foil container.
Place on a plate or in a shallow dish, if necessary.

Quantity	Time on Medium-Low (all power outputs)
1 × 20 cm/8 in pie	4 mins

Standing time: 5 minutes.

Reheating: Turn the microwave output to Full Power.
Pierce the top crust in several places with a sharp knife.

Quantity	Time on Full Power			
	600–650w	700–750w	800–850w	900–1000w
1 × 20 cm/8 in	4–5 mins	3½–4½ mins	3–4 mins	3–3½ mins

Heat just until the pastry (paste) feels warm – the filling will
be much hotter and it must be piping hot before serving.
Don't overheat or the pastry will become very soggy. If this
happens, crisp under a preheated grill (broiler).

Standing time: 5 minutes.

Mince pies, vol-au-vents and individual fruit pies

Defrosting: Arrange in a circle on a plate
after removing any foil containers.

Quantity	Time on Medium-Low (all power outputs)
1	30 secs
2	45 secs
3	1 min
4	1½ mins

Standing time: 5 minutes.

Reheating: Arrange in a circle on the turntable
or a plate after removing any foil containers.

Quantity	Time on Medium (all power outputs)
1	15–20 secs
2	30–40 secs
3	45–50 secs
4	1 min

Heat only until the pastry (paste) feels warm – the filling will be much
hotter. If you overcook them, they will be extremely soggy.

Standing time: 2 minutes.

Sausage rolls

These are best reheated, not just defrosted, before eating.

Defrosting: Arrange in a circle on a plate after removing any wrapping or foil containers. Turn over once during defrosting.

Quantity	Time on Medium-Low (all power outputs)
1 medium	1 min

Standing time: 5 minutes, or until completely defrosted.

Reheating: Place on a piece of kitchen paper (paper towel).

Quantity	Time on Full Power (all power outputs)
1	15–20 secs
2	30–40 secs
3	45–50 secs
4	1 min

To re-crisp the pastry (paste), place briefly under a hot grill (broiler).

Standing time: 1 minute.

Pizza

Defrosting: Remove all packaging and place on a microwave rack.

Quantity	Time on Medium-Low (all power outputs)
1 × 20 cm/ 8 in pizza	4 mins

Standing time: 5 minutes.

Reheating: For a crisp base, cook on a browning dish or place on a microwave rack so that steam can circulate and stop the base getting too soggy.

For slices, test after 10 seconds. Do not overcook.

Quantity	Time on Full Power			
	600–650w	700–750w	800–850w	900–1000w
1 × 20 cm/ 8 in pizza 1 slice	6 mins 20–25 secs	4½ mins 15–20 secs	3 mins 15 secs	2½–3 mins 15 secs

Standing time: 2 minutes.

Chinese take-away

Reheating: Turn into containers and cover. Stir frequently to distribute the heat evenly. You can heat up to 4 separate portions successfully.

Quantity	Time on Full Power			
	600–650w	700–750w	800–850w	900–1000w
1 portion	3½ mins	2½–3 mins	2–2½ mins	1½–2 mins
2 portions	6 mins	5 mins	4 mins	3 mins
3 portions	9 mins	8 mins	7 mins	6–6½ mins
4 portions	12 mins	11 mins	10 mins	9–9½ mins

Standing time: 2 minutes, covered with a dome of foil, shiny side in.

Stir and serve.

Pancakes

Reheating: Place in a stack on kitchen paper (paper towels) on a plate. Cover with more kitchen paper. Alternatively, wrap in a clean napkin.

Turn the stack over halfway through heating time.

Quantity	Time on Full Power			
	600–650w	700–750w	800–850w	900–1000w
1	10–15 secs	10 secs	10 secs	10 secs
8	1½ mins	1–1½ mins	1 min	½–1 min

Standing time: 1 minute.

Serve immediately.

Soups and Sauces

The microwave really comes into its own for defrosting and reheating soups, and making sauces. Soup can be heated and served in the same bowls or mugs. If it is frozen, you can defrost it in its storage container, then transfer to serving dishes to heat fully. Make sure you stir often so that it is piping hot throughout, never just warm in places. Empty canned soups into bowls and reheat in the same way.

Defrosting and reheating times for soups

Defrosting: Leave in the freezer container.
Break up as soon as possible and stir frequently.

Quantity	Time on Medium-Low (all power outputs)
300 ml/½ pt/ 1¼ cups	8–12 mins
600 ml/1 pt/ 2½ cups	12–15 mins

Reheating: Pour into individual mugs or bowls.
Stir twice during heating.

Quantity	Time on Full Power			
	600–650w	700–750w	800–850w	900–1000w
1 portion	2–3 mins	1½–2½ mins	1–2 mins	1–1½ mins
2 portions	3–4 mins	2½–3½ mins	2–3 mins	2–2½ mins
3 portions	4–5 mins	3½–4½ mins	3–4 mins	3–3½ mins
4 portions	5–6 mins	4½–5 mins	4–5 mins	3½–4 mins

Standing time: None.

Stir well before serving and check the soup is piping hot.
Thick, chunky soups may take a little longer than the times given.
Heat a little longer if necessary.

Making sauces

Sauces can be made quickly and easily and you'll never be left with horrible pans to clean. The key to good microwave sauce-making is to remember to stir often so the sauce doesn't go lumpy. A wire whisk is a good 'stirrer' as it helps prevent lumps, but never leave it in the bowl while cooking. Have a spoon rest beside the cooker to put it on between whiskings, so it doesn't drip all over your worktop.

Gravy

All gravies – even for the Sunday roast – can be made in the microwave. Pour any meat juices into a measuring jug and make up to 300 ml/½ pt/1¼ cups with stock or vegetable water. Mix 15–30 ml/1–2 tbsp cornflour (cornstarch) with a little water and stir in thoroughly. Cook on Full Power until bubbling and thickened, stirring after every minute. Season to taste.

Egg-based sauces

Egg-based sauces are easier to make in the microwave than by conventional means. The trick is not to cook them for too long or allow them to boil between whiskings or the mixture will curdle.

Hollandaise sauce: Cut 100 g/4 oz/½ cup butter into small pieces and place in a large bowl. Cover with a sheet of kitchen paper (paper towel) and microwave on Medium for 30–50 seconds or until almost melted. Stir to complete the melting. Add 30 ml/2 tbsp lemon juice and 2 eggs. Whisk until thoroughly blended, then microwave on Full Power for 1 minute. Whisk again. Continue to microwave, whisking every 15 seconds, until thickened, smooth and glossy. Season to taste and serve.

To reheat sauces and gravy

Pour into a serving jug or bowl. Microwave on Medium-High for 2–5 minutes, whisking once or twice until boiling. (If the sauce is not smooth, e.g. tomato, onion or meat sauce, stir with a spoon rather than whisking.) Whisk or stir once more and serve. If the sauce is very thick, whisk in a dash of milk (for milk-based sauces) or water (for gravy, meat or tomato sauces).

Cooking times for sauces

Basic white sauce

Cooking: Using your usual quantities, blend the cornflour (cornstarch) with a little milk, then blend in the remaining milk. Add the butter or margarine.

Stir every minute during cooking until boiling and thickened. Once boiling, cook for a further 1 minute.

Quantity	Time on Full Power			
	600–650w	700–750w	800–850w	900–1000w
300 ml/½ pt/ 1¼ cups	4 mins	3½ mins	3 mins	2½–3 mins

Standing time: None.

Stir well and add salt and pepper to taste for a savoury sauce or sugar for a sweet sauce.

Traditional white sauce

Cooking: Using the quantities for your usual recipe, melt the butter or margarine in a bowl in the microwave on Full Power for 30–40 seconds. Blend in the plain (all-purpose) flour, then gradually whisk in the milk. Return to the microwave.

Whisk every minute during cooking until boiling and thickened. Once boiling, cook for a further 1 minute.

Quantity	Time on Full Power			
	600–650w	700–750w	800–850w	900–1000w
300 ml/½ pt/ 1¼ cups	4 mins	3½ mins	3 mins	2½–3 mins

Standing time: None.

Stir well and add salt and pepper to taste for a savoury sauce or sugar for a sweet sauce.

Flavoured sauces

Both the Basic White Sauce and the Traditional White Sauce recipes (opposite) are suitable for flavoured sauces, although generally sweet sauces are best made with Basic White Sauce as the cornflour (cornstarch) gives a lighter and smoother result. For the quantities given opposite, add the flavourings as follows:

Cheese sauce: Whisk in 50 g/2 oz/½ cup grated Cheddar cheese before seasoning with salt and pepper.

Parsley sauce: Whisk in 30 ml/2 tbsp chopped fresh parsley before seasoning with salt and pepper.

Chocolate sauce: Substitute half of the cornflour (cornstarch) with cocoa (unsweetened chocolate) powder and add 15–30 ml/ 1–2 tbsp caster (superfine) sugar, to taste.

Vanilla sauce: Add vanilla essence (extract) and 15–30 ml/ 1–2 tbsp caster (superfine) sugar, to taste.

Custard: Use custard powder instead of cornflour (cornstarch), add 15–30 ml/1–2 tbsp caster (superfine) sugar and omit the butter or margarine.

Onion sauce: Cook a chopped onion in a bowl in the microwave with a knob of butter or margarine for 2–3 minutes on Full Power until softened. Stir in the flour or cornflour (cornstarch) and milk and continue as opposite, omitting the butter or margarine as you've already added it with the onion.

Other sauces

Tomato sauce: Cook a chopped onion in a bowl with a knob of butter or margarine on Full Power for 2–3 minutes, stirring twice. Add 400 g/15 oz/1 large can of chopped tomatoes, a squeeze of tomato purée (paste), a pinch of caster (superfine) sugar and a pinch of dried basil or oregano. Microwave on Full Power for up to 5 minutes until bubbling and slightly reduced. Season to taste. Use as required.

Meat sauce (e.g. Bolognese): Use your usual recipe. Cook the minced (ground) meat and onion in a bowl, stirring every minute until the grains are separate and no longer pink. Add all the remaining ingredients except the salt and cook on Full Power for 15–20 minutes until rich and thick, stirring every few minutes. Season to taste.

Golden syrup sauce: Spoon golden (light corn) syrup into a jug and microwave on Medium until runny and bubbling very gently round the edges. Do not allow to boil. Add a dash of lemon juice, if liked.

Caramel syrup: Place 90 ml/6 tbsp granulated sugar in a large bowl or jug and stir in 30 ml/2 tbsp water. Microwave on Full Power for 3–6 minutes or until golden brown. Remove with care as the bowl will be extremely hot. Stir in 150 ml/¼ pt/⅔ cup boiling water (take care as it will splutter) and stir until it forms a syrup. If necessary, return to the microwave for 1 minute and stir again to dissolve the caramel.

Jam sauce: Heat equal quantities of jam (conserve) and water in a jug on Full Power, stirring once or twice until melted and hot. Spike with a squeeze of lemon juice if liked. Serve with sponge puddings or over fruit with ice cream.

Eggs and Dairy Products

ontrary to popular belief, eggs cook beautifully in a microwave – but a little care must be taken not to overcook them. You can prepare them in many ways: baked, fried (sautéed), scrambled, poached or as omelettes. You can even make meringues in a quite bizarre way. However, you should not try to boil eggs in their shells or they will explode – you need to buy a special microwave egg-boiler.

Cheese needs a little care, too, but it can be ripened, made into wonderful, smooth sauces and fondues and cooked on toast in seconds. Milk puddings are an absolute delight when microwaved – creamy, delicate and with not a sticky saucepan in sight.

Microwave tips for egg and dairy dishes

In addition to the techniques I describe later in this chapter, there are numerous ways you can use your microwave to save time and effort when cooking with eggs and dairy products.

To unmould mousses

Put the set mousse in its mould in the microwave. Cook on Medium-Low for 20–40 seconds, then invert on a serving plate and lift off the mould.

This method can only be used for mousses in glass or plastic moulds, not metal.

To defrost mousses

Don't try to defrost completely. Microwave on Medium-Low for 2–3 minutes only, then leave to stand to defrost completely at room temperature.

To soften ice-cream
This is not suitable for soft-scoop. Put a 1 litre/1¾ pt/4¼ cup block or tub of hard ice cream in the microwave and loosen the lid, if necessary. Microwave on Medium-Low for 1½ to 2 minutes. 500 ml/ 17 fl oz/1 medium carton will take only 15–20 seconds. Leave to stand for 2 minutes before serving.

To loosen an ice-cream bombe for turning out
Place the bombe in the microwave and cook on Medium-Low for 20–30 seconds, then turn out.
  This method is not suitable for bombes made in metal containers.

To ripen cheese
This is particularly useful for Camembert, Brie and blue cheese. Place on a plate. Microwave on Medium-Low for 15 seconds to 1 minute, depending on the size of the cheese and how unripe it is, until the cheese is just soft, not running. Leave to stand for 5 minutes before serving.

To soften fresh soft cheeses or cheese spreads
Remove all foil coverings and place in the microwave in the container and cook on Medium-Low for 5–15 seconds only. Leave to stand for 1 minute before spreading.

To defrost frozen whipped or double (heavy) cream
First remove any foil from the container. For a 250 ml/9 fl oz/ medium carton, microwave on Medium-Low for 2½ to 3 minutes. Leave to stand for 5 minutes, then stir gently and serve.

To soften butter or margarine
Put on a plate. Heat on Medium-Low for about 30 seconds for each 100 g/4 oz/½ cup. Do not let it start to melt completely.

Eggs

If you like firm yolks, cook for a few seconds more. Remember, they will continue to cook on standing.

Note: For 900–1000 watt cookers, you may find it best to cook eggs on Medium-High instead of Full Power.

Baked eggs
For all power outputs: In each of the ramekins (custard cups) you wish to use, melt a small knob of butter or margarine for a few seconds on Full Power in the microwave. Break an egg into each dish. Prick the yolks in two or three places with a cocktail stick (toothpick) to prevent bursting. Top each with 5 ml/1 tsp double (heavy) or whipping cream. Arrange the ramekins in a circle in the microwave. Bake for 15 seconds per egg on Full Power. Stand for 1 minute, then bake again for a further 20 seconds. Leave to stand again before serving.

Fried (sautéed) eggs
You can use a browning dish (see page 22) for this, or oil or lightly butter a saucer. Break an egg on the dish or saucer and pierce the yolk two or three times with a cocktail stick (toothpick). Cover with a plate. Cook on Full Power for 30 seconds. Leave to stand for 1 minute. Cook for a further 15–30 seconds or until the white is just set. Leave to stand for 1 minute to complete cooking.

For 2 eggs: Use an oiled or greased shallow dish. Cook as above for 1 minute on Full Power, stand for 1 minute, then cook for a further 20–40 seconds until the whites are just set. Don't try to fry more than two eggs at once.

Poached eggs
For all power outputs: Put about 2.5 cm/1 in boiling water in up to four ramekin dishes (custard cups). Break an egg into each. Pierce the yolks in two or three places with a cocktail stick (toothpick). Place in a circle in the microwave. Cook on Full Power for 30 seconds per egg. Leave to stand for 2 minutes to complete cooking, then carefully drain off the water before serving.

Scrambled eggs

Use up to 8 eggs. Break in a bowl and beat well. Beat in 15–30 ml/1–2 tbsp milk per egg. Add a knob of butter or margarine and a little salt and pepper. Microwave on Full Power for 45 seconds to 1 minute **per egg**, stirring after each minute. Remove from the oven while still slightly runny, as the eggs will continue to cook. Leave to stand for 2 minutes before serving. Take care not to overcook. More eggs take less time per egg, so check frequently.

Omelettes

Melt a small knob of butter or margarine in a small, round, shallow dish for a few seconds on Full Power. Beat 3 eggs with a good pinch of salt and pepper and 30 ml/2 tbsp cold water until just blended, not frothy. Pour into the dish. Cover with a plate. Cook on Full Power for 1½ minutes. Stir gently to bring the cooked mixture towards the centre. Cook again for 1 further minute. Remove the plate and cook for a further 30 seconds to 1½ minutes, if necessary, until completely set. Fold over, slide out of the dish and serve. Serves 1.

You can add flavourings – such as grated cheese, herbs, fried (sautéed) mushrooms, etc. – in your usual way, after the first 1½ minutes of cooking time.

Soufflé omelettes

Separate 4 eggs. Beat the yolks with 30 ml/2 tbsp water. Season with a little salt and pepper or sweeten with 5 ml/1 tsp caster (superfine) sugar. Whisk the egg whites until stiff and fold in with a metal spoon. Lightly butter a 20 cm/8 in round, shallow dish. Spoon in the egg mixture. Cook on Medium for 5–8 minutes, until puffy and just set. Fold in half and serve straight away, either plain or with a savoury or sweet sauce of your choice. Serves 2.

Egg custard

Whisk 3 eggs with 30 ml/2 tbsp caster (superfine) sugar and 450 ml/¾ pt/2 cups milk. Add a few drops of vanilla essence (extract), to taste. Pour into four ramekins (custard cups) and stand these in a large, shallow, round dish. Pour enough hot water into the large dish to come halfway up the sides of the ramekins.

Alternatively, put all the mixture in a 20 cm/8 in round dish. Cook on Medium for 16–20 minutes until the custard is set. Serve hot or leave to cool, then chill for at least 3 hours or preferably overnight before turning out and serving. Serves 4.

Crème caramel

To make the caramel, put 90 ml/6 tbsp granulated sugar and 30 ml/2 tbsp hot water in a bowl. Stir well. Microwave on Full Power for 3–6 minutes until golden brown. Pour into four ramekin dishes (custard cups), then continue as for Egg Custard (above). Serves 4.

Meringues

Microwaved meringues look wonderful – pure white and crisp. The downside is you have to use an enormous amount of sugar. On the other hand, this method takes very little time or fuel and a single egg white goes a long way!

Whisk 1 egg white until frothy but not stiff. Gradually beat in 350 g/12 oz/2 cups sifted icing (confectioners') sugar. When the mixture becomes stiff, knead in the remaining sugar until the mixture forms a stiff paste. Cut in half and roll out each half to a sausage shape. Cut each sausage into 12 pieces and roll into balls. Place six in a circle on a sheet of non-stick baking parchment on a plate. Microwave on Full Power for 1¼–2½ minutes until crisp and dry. Remove from the microwave, leave to stand for 5 minutes, then transfer to a wire rack to cool completely. Repeat with the remaining batches of meringues. Store in an airtight container. Serve with desserts, or sandwich together in pairs with cream.

Pavlova

Prepare the meringue mixture as above. Divide in half and roll each half into an 18 cm/7 in round. Hollow the centre slightly. Microwave on Full Power for 2 minutes. Leave to stand for 1 minute, then microwave again for 2 minutes until crisp and dry. Leave to stand for 5 minutes, then transfer to a wire rack to cool. Repeat with the remaining half. Top with cream and fruit when cold.

Cheese

Cheese on toast
Make the toast in the usual way and spread with butter or margarine, if liked. Place on a plate. Top with an even layer of thinly sliced or grated cheese. Microwave on Full Power for 15–45 seconds, until the cheese has just melted. Do not overcook or the whole thing will become hard.

Cheese fondue
Use your usual recipe but heat the liquid in a large bowl on Full Power until hot but not boiling. Mix all the remaining ingredients together and gradually blend into the hot liquid. Microwave on Full Power, stirring every 2 minutes until smooth and bubbling.

Milk and cream

Milk puddings
Creamy rice, semolina (cream of wheat), tapioca and sago can be made quickly and easily in the microwave, using your usual recipe. For best results, follow these guidelines.

- Use a very large dish to prevent boiling over.

- Put the rice, semolina, etc. in the dish with the sugar and milk and stir well.

- Cook on Full Power until the milk boils. Stir again.

- Turn down to Medium and continue cooking for 10–40 minutes (depending on the grain), stirring two or three times, until the pudding is creamy and the grains are soft. The longer you cook, the creamer it will be.

- Sprinkle with grated nutmeg, if liked, before serving.

Fish

ish of all kinds can be cooked to perfection in the microwave, keeping it moist and full of flavour. It cooks very quickly, however, so great care must be taken not to overdo it. This is especially true of shellfish.

General rules for cooking fish

• Remove the fish from the oven when the larger flakes are still translucent. Cover and leave to stand for a few minutes and the fish will complete cooking.

• Slash whole fish in two or three places on each side before cooking to ensure even distribution of the microwaves.

• Use the same method for smoked fish as for plain fish.

• Cover thin tails with a small strip of smooth foil to protect against overcooking.

• Do not add salt before cooking.

Frozen fish

Fish can be cooked from frozen, but cook on Medium instead of Full Power, allowing an extra 1–2 minutes per 450 g/1 lb.

Fillets/tail pieces
Defrost, if time allows, then skin before cooking, if liked. Lay the fish in a shallow dish in single layer, with the thinnest parts towards the centre. Either dot with butter or margarine or add 30 ml/2 tbsp liquid (wine, milk, cider, water or stock) per portion. Add a sprig of fresh herbs or a bay leaf, if liked. Cover and microwave on Full Power for the time given for individual entries. Leave to stand for 2 minutes before serving. Carefully lift the fish out of the liquid. If liked, thicken the liquid with a little cornflour (cornstarch), blended with milk or water, cooked on Full Power for

1–2 minutes, stirring once. Add cream or crème fraîche, chopped fresh parsley, capers, prawns (shrimp) or sautéed mushrooms, if liked, and season to taste.

Steaks and cutlets
Prepare as above but remove the bones and stuff the cavity of the cutlets with a stuffing, if liked (you may need to add on an extra few seconds' cooking time to allow for the stuffing).

Whole round fish (trout, mackerel, herring)
Slash in two or three places on each side. Lay head to tail in a shallow dish. Dot with a little butter or margarine and sprinkle with lemon juice. Add herbs, if liked. Cover and cook according to individual entries, carefully turning over once after 3 minutes' cooking time.

Soused mackerel or herring
Use your normal recipe. Place the fish and liquid in a casserole dish (Dutch oven), cover and microwave on Full Power for about 8–12 minutes until the fish feel just tender when pierced with a knife. Rearrange once after 5 minutes. Leave to stand in their liquid until completely cold, then chill before serving.

Whole flat fish (plaice, sole, halibut)
These benefit from being cooked on Medium. Lay in a single layer in a shallow dish or cook one at a time. Dot with butter or margarine and sprinkle with lemon juice. Cover and cook for the time stated in individual entries.

Raw prawns (shrimp) or scallops
These should also be cooked on Medium, as they cook very quickly and if they are overcooked they become very tough. Place in a shallow dish and add a little butter or margarine or liquid (see Fillets/tail pieces, page 49). Cover and cook for the time stated in individual entries, stirring once or twice to distribute the energy evenly. Cook just until turning pink for prawns, or until scallops go milky white. Frozen, cooked seafood can also be defrosted very successfully (see individual entries).

Mussels
Scrub and remove beards, discarding any that are damaged or open. They are best cooked in a little liquid to keep them moist and should be cooked just until they open, no longer, so stir and check after every minute. Discard any that remain closed.

Crab and lobster
Do not cook live crab or lobster in the microwave. You can defrost blocks of frozen crab or lobster meat in the same way as minced (ground) meat (see page 83).

Roes
Prick the membranes of 225 g/8 oz roes in several places. Lay in a single layer in a lightly buttered or oiled dish. Cover and cook on Full Power for 1½–3 minutes. Turn over and cook for a further 1–3 minutes or until cooked through. Season, leave to stand for 2 minutes and serve, sprinkled with lemon juice and chopped fresh parsley.

Fish cakes
Cook from frozen. Place in a circle on a lightly oiled plate. Cover and cook on Full Power for 45 seconds to 1¼ minutes per cake, turning once. Crisp under a preheated grill (broiler) briefly, if liked, or use a browning dish (see pages 22–3).

Fish fingers
These can be cooked from frozen but the coating will be soft, not crisp. Arrange in a circle on a lightly oiled plate. Microwave on Full Power for 30 seconds to 1 minute per fish finger, turning once. Crisp briefly under a hot grill (broiler), if liked, or – better – use a browning dish (see pages 22–3).

Defrosting and cooking times for fish

If you have time, it is always best to defrost frozen fish before cooking in the microwave, rather than cooking from frozen, as it will cook more evenly. In this section, I have given you times for almost every type of fish you are likely to cook. Thick pieces may need a little extra cooking time.

Cod fillets

Defrosting: Arrange with the thinnest parts towards the centre on a microwave rack over a plate. Cover with a plate, lid or greaseproof (waxed) paper.

If in a block, separate as soon as possible and arrange as before.

Quantity	Time on Medium-Low (all power outputs)
225 g/8 oz	3 mins
450 g/1 lb	5–6 mins

Standing time: 5 minutes, covered with a dome of foil, shiny side in.

Cooking: Arrange in a single layer in a shallow dish, thinnest parts overlapping towards the centre. Brush with melted butter, or pour on a little milk, wine, stock or water, and add other flavourings of your choice. Cover with a lid, greaseproof (waxed) paper or clingfilm (plastic wrap), rolled back slightly at one edge.

Check thinner parts are not overcooking. If so, cover with a thin strip of foil to prevent further cooking.

Quantity	Time on Full Power			
	600–650w	700–750w	800–850w	900–1000w
225 g/8 oz	2–2½ mins	1½–2 mins	1½ mins	1–1½ mins
450 g/1 lb	3½–4 mins	3–3½ mins	2½–3 mins	2–2½ mins

Standing time: 2 minutes, covered with a dome of foil, shiny side in.

Smoked cod fillets
See **Smoked haddock fillets** (page 55).

Cod steaks/cutlets

Defrosting: Arrange with the thinnest parts towards the centre on a microwave rack over a plate. Cover with a plate, lid or greaseproof (waxed) paper.

If in a block, separate as soon as possible and arrange as before.

Quantity	Time on Medium-Low (all power outputs)
225 g/8 oz	3 mins
450 g/1 lb	5–6 mins

Standing time: 5 minutes, covered with a dome of foil, shiny side in.

Cooking: Arrange in a single layer in a shallow dish, thinnest parts towards the centre. Brush with melted butter, or pour in a little milk, wine, stock or water, and add other flavourings of your choice. For cutlets, remove the bone and stuff the cavity, if liked. Cover with a lid, greaseproof (waxed) paper or clingfilm (plastic wrap), rolled back slightly at one edge.

Allow a little extra cooking time per cutlet if stuffed or very thick.

Quantity	Time on Full Power			
	600–650w	700–750w	800–850w	900–1000w
225 g/8 oz	2–2½ mins	1½–2 mins	1½ mins	1–1½ mins
450 g/1 lb	3½–4 mins	3–3½ mins	2½–3 mins	2–2½ mins

Standing time: 2 minutes, covered with a dome of foil, shiny side in.

Boil-in-the-bag cod

Cook from frozen. The portions come in various sizes so follow manufacturer's instructions, if there are any, or cook as follows.

Cooking: Pierce the frozen bag and place on a plate.

Using oven-gloved hands, shake the bag gently once or twice during cooking.

Quantity	Time on Medium			
	600–650w	700–750w	800–850w	900–1000w
225 g/8 oz	5 mins	4 mins	3½ mins	3–3½ mins

Standing time: 5 minutes, covered with a dome of foil, shiny side in.

Haddock fillets

Defrosting: Arrange with the thinnest parts towards the centre
on a microwave rack over a plate. Cover with a plate, lid
or greaseproof (waxed) paper.

If in a block, separate as soon as possible and arrange as before.

Quantity	Time on Medium-Low (all power outputs)
225 g/8 oz	3 mins
450 g/1 lb	5–6 mins

Standing time: 5 minutes, covered with a dome of foil, shiny side in.

Cooking: Arrange in a single layer in a shallow dish
with the thinnest parts overlapping towards the centre. Brush with
melted butter, or pour in a little milk, wine, stock or water, and add other
flavourings of your choice. Cover with a lid, greaseproof (waxed) paper or
clingfilm (plastic wrap), rolled back slightly at one edge.

Check thinner parts are not overcooking. If so, cover with a thin strip of
foil to prevent further cooking.

Quantity	Time on Full Power			
	600–650w	700–750w	800–850w	900–1000w
225 g/8 oz	2–2½ mins	1½–2 mins	1½ mins	1–1½ mins
450 g/1 lb	3½–4 mins	3–3½ mins	2½–3 mins	2–2½ mins

Standing time: 2 minutes, covered with a dome of foil, shiny side in.

Smoked haddock fillets

Defrosting: Arrange with the thinnest parts towards the centre
on a microwave rack over a plate. Cover with a plate, lid
or greaseproof (waxed) paper.

If in a block, separate as soon as possible and arrange as before.

Quantity	Time on Medium-Low (all power outputs)
225 g/8 oz	3 mins
450 g/1 lb	5–6 mins

Standing time: 5 minutes, covered with a dome of foil, shiny side in.

Cooking: Arrange in a single layer in a shallow dish with the thinnest parts overlapping towards the centre. Brush with melted butter, or pour in a little milk or water. Cover with a lid, greaseproof (waxed) paper or clingfilm (plastic wrap), rolled back slightly at one edge.

Check thinner parts are not overcooking. If so, cover with a thin strip of foil to prevent further cooking.

Quantity	Time on Full Power			
	600–650w	700–750w	800–850w	900–1000w
225 g/8 oz	2–2½ mins	1½–2 mins	1½ mins	1–1½ mins
450 g/1 lb	3½–4 mins	3–3½ mins	2½–3 mins	2–2½ mins

Boil-in-the-bag haddock

Cook from frozen. The portions come in various sizes so follow manufacturer's instructions, if there are any, or cook as follows.

Cooking: Pierce the frozen bag and place on a plate. Using oven-gloved hands, shake the bag gently once or twice during cooking.

Quantity	Time on Medium			
	600–650w	700–750w	800–850w	900–1000w
225 g/8 oz	5 mins	4 mins	3½ mins	3–3½ mins

Standing time: 5 minutes, covered with a dome of foil, shiny side in.

Hake steaks
See **Cod steaks/cutlets** (page 52).

Herring fillets

Defrosting: Arrange with the thinnest parts towards the centre on a microwave rack over a plate. Cover with a plate, lid or greaseproof (waxed) paper.

If in a block, separate as soon as possible and arrange as before.

Quantity	Time on Medium-Low (all power outputs)
225 g/8 oz	3 mins
450 g/1 lb	5–6 mins

Standing time: 5 minutes, covered with a dome of foil, shiny side in.

Cooking: Arrange in a single layer in a shallow dish with the thinnest parts overlapping towards the centre. Brush with melted butter, or pour in a little wine, stock or water, and add other flavourings of your choice. Cover with a lid, greaseproof (waxed) paper or clingfilm (plastic wrap), rolled back slightly at one edge.

Check thinner parts are not overcooking. If so, cover with a thin strip of foil to prevent further cooking.

Quantity	Time on Full Power			
	600–650w	700–750w	800–850w	900–1000w
225 g/8 oz	2–2½ mins	1½–2 mins	1½ mins	1–1½ mins
450 g/1 lb	3½–4 mins	3–3½ mins	2½–3 mins	2–2½ mins

Standing time: 2 minutes, covered with a dome of foil, shiny side in.

Whole herring

Defrosting: Place up to two at a time head to tail on a microwave rack over a plate. Cover the tail ends with a thin strip of foil. Cover the fish with a plate, lid or greaseproof (waxed) paper.

Quantity	Time on Medium-Low (all power outputs)
1	3–4 mins
2	6–8 mins

Standing time: 5 minutes, covered with a dome of foil, shiny side in.

Cooking: Clean, rinse and trim fins and tail. Make several slashes in each side of the body. Place head to tail in a shallow dish. Brush with melted butter, or pour in a little wine, stock or water, and add other flavourings of your choice. Cover with a lid, greaseproof (waxed) paper or clingfilm (plastic wrap), rolled back slightly at one edge. Alternatively, wrap individually in a double thickness of greaseproof paper.

Check thinner parts are not overcooking. If so, cover with a thin strip of foil to prevent further cooking.

Quantity	Time on Full Power			
	600–650w	700–750w	800–850w	900–1000w
1	4 mins	3½ mins	3 mins	2½–3 mins
2	5–6 mins	4–4½ mins	3½–4 mins	3–3½ mins

Standing time: 2 minutes, covered with a dome of foil, shiny side in.

Whole kippers

Defrosting: Place on a microwave rack over a plate. Cover with a plate, lid or greaseproof (waxed) paper.

Quantity	Time on Medium-Low (all power outputs)
1	3 mins

Standing time: 5 minutes, covered with a dome of foil, shiny side in.

Cooking: Cook one at a time. Place in a shallow dish. Brush with melted butter, or add a little water. Cover with a lid, greaseproof (waxed) paper or clingfilm (plastic wrap), rolled back slightly at one edge.

Quantity	Time on Full Power			
	600–650w	700–750w	800–850w	900–1000w
1	3 mins	2½ mins	2 mins	1½–2 mins

Standing time: 2 minutes, covered with a dome of foil, shiny side in.

Kipper fillets

Defrosting: Arrange with the thinnest parts towards the centre on a microwave rack over a plate. Cover with a plate, lid or greaseproof (waxed) paper.

If in a block, separate as soon as possible and arrange as before.

Quantity	Time on Medium-Low (all power outputs)
225 g/8 oz	3 mins
450 g/1 lb	5–6 mins

Standing time: 5 minutes, covered with a dome of foil, shiny side in.

Cooking: Arrange in a single layer in a shallow dish, thinnest parts overlapping towards the centre. Brush with melted butter, or pour in a little water, and add other flavourings of your choice. Cover with a lid, greaseproof (waxed) paper or clingfilm (plastic wrap), rolled back slightly at one edge.

Check thinner parts are not overcooking. If so, cover with a thin strip of foil to prevent further cooking.

Quantity	Time on Full Power			
	600–650w	700–750w	800–850w	900–1000w
225 g/8 oz	2–2½ mins	1½–2 mins	1½ mins	1–1½ mins
450 g/1 lb	3½–4 mins	3–3½ mins	2½–3 mins	2–2½ mins

Standing time: 2 minutes, covered with a dome of foil, shiny side in.

Boil-in-the-bag kippers

Cook from frozen. The packs come in various sizes so follow manufacturer's instructions if there are any, or cook as follows.

Cooking: Pierce the frozen bag and place on a plate. Using oven-gloved hands, shake the bag gently once or twice during cooking.

Quantity	Time on Medium			
	600–650w	700–750w	800–850w	900–1000w
225 g/8 oz	5 mins	4 mins	3½ mins	3–3½ mins

Standing time: 5 minutes, covered with a dome of foil, shiny side in.

Huss steaks
See **Cod steaks/fillets** (page 52).

Mackerel fillets

Defrosting: Arrange with the thinnest parts towards the centre on a microwave rack over a plate. Cover with a plate, lid or greaseproof (waxed) paper.

If in a block, separate as soon as possible and arrange as before.

Quantity	Time on Medium-Low (all power outputs)
225 g/8 oz	3 mins
450 g/1 lb	5–6 mins

Standing time: 5 minutes, covered with a dome of foil, shiny side in.

Cooking: Arrange in a single layer in a shallow dish, thinnest parts overlapping towards the centre. Brush with melted butter, or pour in a little wine, stock or water, and add other flavourings of your choice. Cover with a lid, greaseproof (waxed) paper or clingfilm (plastic wrap), rolled back slightly at one edge.

Check thinner parts are not overcooking. If so, cover with a thin strip of foil to prevent further cooking.

Quantity	Time on Full Power			
	600–650w	700–750w	800–850w	900–1000w
225 g/8 oz	2–2½ mins	1½–2 mins	1½ mins	1–1½ mins
450 g/1 lb	3½–4 mins	3–3½ mins	2½–3 mins	2–2½ mins

Standing time: 2 minutes, covered with a dome of foil, shiny side in.

Whole mackerel

Defrosting: Place up to two at a time head to tail on a microwave rack over a plate. Cover the tail ends with a thin strip of foil. Cover the fish with a plate, lid or greaseproof (waxed) paper.

Quantity	Time on Medium-Low (all power outputs)
1	3–4 mins
2	6–8 mins

Standing time: 5 minutes, covered with a dome of foil, shiny side in.

Cooking: Clean, rinse and trim fins and tail. Make several slashes in both sides of the body. Place head to tail in a shallow dish. Brush with melted butter, or pour in a little wine, stock or water, and add other flavourings of your choice. Cover with a lid, greaseproof (waxed) paper or clingfilm (plastic wrap), rolled back slightly at one edge. Alternatively, flavour as before and wrap individually in a double thickness of greaseproof paper.

Check thinner parts are not overcooking. If so, cover with a thin strip of foil to prevent further cooking.

Quantity	Time on Full Power			
	600–650w	700–750w	800–850w	900–1000w
1	4 mins	3½ mins	3 mins	2½–3 mins
2	5–6 mins	4–4½ mins	3½–4 mins	3–3½ mins

Standing time: 2 minutes, covered with a dome of foil, shiny side in.

Smoked mackerel fillets
See **Kipper fillets** (page 57).

Whole smoked mackerel

Defrosting: Place up to two at a time, head to tail, on a microwave rack over a plate. Cover the tail ends with a thin strip of foil. Cover the fish with a plate, lid or greaseproof (waxed) paper.

Quantity	Time on Medium-Low (all power outputs)
1	3–4 mins
2	6–8 mins

Standing time: 5 minutes, covered with a dome of foil, shiny side in.

Cooking: Place head to tail in a shallow dish. Brush with melted butter. Cover with a lid, greaseproof (waxed) paper or clingfilm (plastic wrap), rolled back slightly at one edge. Alternatively, flavour as before and wrap individually in a double thickness of greaseproof paper.

Check thinner parts are not overcooking. If so, cover with a thin strip of foil to prevent further cooking.

Quantity	Time on Full Power			
	600–650w	700–750w	800–850w	900–1000w
1	4 mins	3½ mins	3 mins	2½–3 mins
2	5–6 mins	4–4½ mins	3½–4 mins	3–3½ mins

Standing time: 2 minutes, covered with a dome of foil, shiny side in.

Monkfish

Defrosting: Arrange with the thinnest parts towards the centre on a microwave rack over a plate. Cover with a plate, lid or greaseproof (waxed) paper.

If in a block, separate as soon as possible and arrange as before.

Quantity	Time on Medium-Low (all power outputs)
225 g/8 oz	3 mins
450 g/1 lb	5–6 mins

Standing time: 5 minutes, covered with a dome of foil, shiny side in.

Cooking: Arrange in a single layer in a shallow dish, thinnest parts overlapping towards the centre. Brush with melted butter, or pour in a little milk, wine, stock or water, and add other flavourings of your choice. Cover with a lid, greaseproof (waxed) paper or clingfilm (plastic wrap), rolled back slightly at one edge.

Check thinner parts are not overcooking. If so, cover with a thin strip of foil to prevent further cooking.

Alternatively, cut into cubes, marinate, thread on soaked wooden skewers, then place in a shallow dish or on a microwave rack over a plate. Brush with more marinade and cook as below, turning once halfway through cooking.

Quantity	Time on Full Power			
	600–650w	700–750w	800–850w	900–1000w
225 g/8 oz	2–2½ mins	1½–2 mins	1½ mins	1–1½ mins
450 g/1 lb	3½–4 mins	3–3½ mins	2½–3 mins	2–2½ mins

Standing time: 2 minutes, covered with a dome of foil, shiny side in.

Mussels

Defrosting: If bought frozen, defrost according to the instructions on the packet.

Cooking: Scrub and remove beards, discarding any that are damaged or open. Place in a large casserole dish (Dutch oven) with 150 ml/¼ pt/ 2⅔ cups water or white wine. Cover. Stir after every minute until the shells are open. Discard any that remain closed.

Quantity	Time on Full Power			
	600–650w	700–750w	800–850w	900–1000w
1 kg/2¼ lb	5–7 mins	4–6 mins	3–4 mins	3 mins

Standing time: 2 minutes, covered with a dome of foil, shiny side in.

Plaice fillets

Defrosting: Arrange with the thinnest parts towards the centre on a microwave rack over a plate. Cover with a plate, lid or greaseproof (waxed) paper.

If in a block, separate as soon as possible and arrange as before.

Quantity	Time on Medium-Low (all power outputs)
225 g/8 oz	3 mins
450 g/1 lb	5–6 mins

Standing time: 5 minutes, covered with a dome of foil, shiny side in.

Cooking: Arrange in a single layer in a shallow dish, thinnest parts overlapping towards the centre or rolled up. Brush with melted butter, or pour in a little milk, wine, stock or water, and add other flavourings of your choice. Cover with a lid, greaseproof (waxed) paper or clingfilm (plastic wrap), rolled back slightly at one edge.

Check thinner parts are not overcooking. If so, cover with a thin strip of foil to prevent further cooking.

Quantity	Time on Full Power			
	600–650w	700–750w	800–850w	900–1000w
225 g/8 oz	2–2½ mins	1½–2 mins	1½ mins	1–1½ mins
450 g/1 lb	3½–4 mins	3–3½ mins	2½–3 mins	2–2½ mins

Standing time: 2 minutes, covered with a dome of foil, shiny side in.

Whole plaice

Defrosting: Put two at a time on a microwave rack over a plate. Cover with a plate, lid or greaseproof (waxed) paper.

Quantity	Time on Medium-Low (all power outputs)
1 fish, about 225 g/8 oz	3 mins

Standing time: 5 minutes, covered with a dome of foil, shiny side in.

Cooking: Put a maximum of two fish side by side in a shallow dish, or cook one at a time. Brush with melted butter, or pour in a little milk, wine, stock or water, and add other flavourings of your choice. Protect the tails with a thin strip of foil. Cover with a lid, greaseproof (waxed) paper or clingfilm (plastic wrap), rolled back slightly at one edge.

Quantity	Time on Full Power			
	600–650w	700–750w	800–850w	900–1000w
1 fish, about 225 g/8 oz	2 mins	1½–2 mins	1½ min	1–1½ mins
1 fish, about 450 g/1 lb	4 mins	3½ mins	3 mins	2½–3 mins

Standing time: 2 minutes, covered with a dome of foil, shiny side in.

Pollack fillets
See **Cod steaks/fillets** (page 52).

Cooked peeled prawns (shrimp)

Defrosting: Spread out on kitchen paper (paper towels) in a single layer in a shallow dish.

Stir gently once or twice during defrosting. Do not allow to become warm.

Quantity	Time on Medium-Low (all power outputs)
225 g/8 oz	2 mins
450 g/1 lb	3–3½ mins

Standing time: 5 minutes, covered with a dome of foil, shiny side in.

Raw prawns (shrimp)

If frozen, do not defrost before cooking. Cook from frozen but add on an extra ½–1 minute to the given cooking times.

Cooking: Arrange in a single layer in a shallow dish.
Brush with melted butter, or pour in a little wine or water, and add other flavourings of your choice. Cover with a lid, greaseproof (waxed) paper or clingfilm (plastic wrap), rolled back slightly at one edge.

Watch carefully as they overcook quickly. Stir gently once during cooking. Cook until just turned pink.

Quantity	Time on Medium			
	600–650w	700–750w	800–850w	900–1000w
225 g/8 oz	2–2½ mins	1½–2 mins	1½ min	1–1½ mins
450 g/1 lb	3–4 mins	2½–3 mins	2–2½ mins	2 mins

Standing time: 2 minutes, covered with a dome of foil, shiny side in.

Whole red or grey mullet

Defrosting: Place up to two at a time, head to tail, on a microwave rack over a plate. Cover the tail ends with a thin strip of foil. Cover the fish with a plate, lid or greaseproof (waxed) paper.

Quantity	Time on Medium-Low (all power outputs)
1	3–4 mins
2	6–8 mins

Standing time: 5 minutes, covered with a dome of foil, shiny side in.

Cooking: Clean, rinse and trim fins and tail. Place head to tail in a shallow dish. Brush with melted butter, or pour in a little stock, water or wine, and add other flavourings of your choice. Cover with a lid, greaseproof (waxed) paper or clingfilm (plastic wrap), rolled back slightly at one edge. Alternatively, flavour as before and wrap individually in a double thickness of greaseproof paper.

Check thinner parts are not overcooking. If so, cover with a thin strip of foil to prevent further cooking.

Quantity	Time on Full Power			
	600–650w	700–750w	800–850w	900–1000w
1	4 mins	3½ mins	3 mins	2½–3 mins
2	5–6 mins	4–4½ mins	3½–4 mins	3–3½ mins

Standing time: 2 minutes, covered with a dome of foil, shiny side in.

Salmon fillets

Defrosting: Arrange with the thinnest parts towards the centre on a microwave rack over a plate. Cover with a plate, lid or greaseproof (waxed) paper.

If in a block, separate as soon as possible and arrange as before.

Quantity	Time on Medium-Low (all power outputs)
225 g/8 oz	3 mins
450 g/1 lb	5–6 mins

Standing time: 5 minutes, covered with a dome of foil, shiny side in.

Cooking: Arrange in a single layer in a shallow dish, thinnest parts overlapping towards the centre. Brush with melted butter, or pour in a little wine or water, and add other flavourings of your choice. Cover with a lid, greaseproof (waxed) paper or clingfilm (plastic wrap), rolled back slightly at one edge.

Check thinner parts are not overcooking. If so, cover with a thin strip of foil to prevent further cooking.

Quantity	Time on Full Power			
	600–650w	700–750w	800–850w	900–1000w
225 g/8 oz	2–2½ mins	1½–2 mins	1½ mins	1–1½ mins
450 g/1 lb	3½–4 mins	3–3½ mins	2½–3 mins	2–2½ mins

Standing time: 2 minutes, covered with a dome of foil, shiny side in.

Salmon steaks or cutlets

Defrosting: Arrange with the thinnest parts towards the centre on a microwave rack over a plate. Cover with a plate, lid or greaseproof (waxed) paper.

If in a block, separate as soon as possible and arrange as before.

Quantity	Time on Medium-Low (all power outputs)
225 g/8 oz	3 mins
450 g/1 lb	5–6 mins

Standing time: 5 minutes, covered with a dome of foil, shiny side in.

Cooking: Arrange in a single layer in a shallow dish, thinnest parts towards the centre. Brush with melted butter, or pour in a little stock, wine or water, and add other flavourings of your choice. For cutlets, remove the bone and stuff the cavity, if liked. Cover with a lid, greaseproof (waxed) paper or clingfilm (plastic wrap), rolled back slightly at one edge.

Allow a little extra cooking time per cutlet if stuffed or very thick.

Quantity	Time on Full Power			
	600–650w	700–750w	800–850w	900–1000w
225 g/8 oz	2–2½ mins	1½–2 mins	1½ mins	1–1½ mins
450 g/1 lb	3½–4 mins	3–3½ mins	2½–3 mins	2–2½ mins

Standing time: 2 minutes, covered with a dome of foil, shiny side in.

Whole salmon

Some salmon are simply too large for the average household microwave, but those weighing up to about 1.75 kg/4 lb cook perfectly. For large fish over 900 g/2 lb, defrost for half the calculated time, leave to stand for 20 minutes, then turn over and finish defrosting.

Defrosting: Only defrost in the microwave if the whole fish can be laid in the oven and turned on the turntable (if you have one) without touching the sides at all.

Place on a microwave rack over a plate. Protect the head and tail with thin strips of foil. Cover with greaseproof (waxed) paper.

Quantity	Time on Medium-Low (all power outputs)
Per 450 g/1 lb	5 mins

Standing time: 5 minutes, covered with a dome of foil, shiny side in.

Cooking: Place in a shallow dish, curling the fish round, if necessary to fit. Brush with melted butter, or add a little wine, stock or water, and other flavourings of your choice. Cover with a lid, greaseproof (waxed) paper or clingfilm (plastic wrap), rolled back slightly at one edge.

Check thinner parts are not overcooking. If so, cover with thin strips of foil to prevent further cooking.

Quantity	Time on Full Power			
	600–650w	700–750w	800–850w	900–1000w
Per 450 g/1 lb	3½–4 mins	3–3½ mins	2½–3 mins	2–2½ mins

Standing time: 5 minutes, covered with a dome of foil, shiny side in.

Scallops

Defrosting: Arrange around a microwave rack over a plate or spread out small (queen) ones in a single layer. Cover with a plate, lid or greaseproof (waxed) paper.

If in a block, separate as soon as possible and arrange around the rack.

Quantity	Time on Medium-Low (all power outputs)
225 g/8 oz 450 g/1 lb	2 mins 3–3½ mins

Standing time: 5 minutes, covered with a dome of foil, shiny side in.

Cooking: Arrange in a single layer in a shallow dish.
Add a little wine, stock, milk or water, and other flavourings of your choice. Cover with a lid, greaseproof (waxed) paper or clingfilm (plastic wrap), rolled back slightly at one edge.

Watch carefully, as they overcook quickly. Turn over large ones and stir queen scallops gently once during cooking. Cook until just milky white.

Quantity	Time on Medium			
	600–650w	700–750w	800–850w	900–1000w
225 g/8 oz 450 g/1 lb	2–2½ mins 3–4 mins	1½–2 mins 2½–3 mins	1½ mins 2–2½ mins	1–1½ mins 2 mins

Standing time: 2 minutes, covered with a dome of foil, shiny side in.

Scampi

Defrosting: Arrange around a microwave rack over a plate. Cover with a plate, lid or greaseproof (waxed) paper.

If in a block, separate as soon as possible and arrange around the rack.

Quantity	Time on Medium-Low (all power outputs)
225 g/8 oz	2 mins
450 g/1 lb	3–3½ mins

Standing time: 5 minutes, covered with a dome of foil, shiny side in.

Cooking: Arrange in a single layer in a shallow dish.
Add a little wine or water, and other flavourings of your choice.
Cover with a lid, greaseproof (waxed) paper or clingfilm (plastic wrap), rolled back slightly at one edge.

Watch carefully, as they overcook quickly. Stir gently once during cooking.

Quantity	Time on Medium			
	600–650w	700–750w	800–850w	900–1000w
225 g/8 oz	2–2½ mins	1½–2 mins	1½ mins	1–1½ mins
450 g/1 lb	3–4 mins	2½–3 mins	2–2½ mins	2 mins

Standing time: 4 minutes, covered with a dome of foil, shiny side in.

Sole fillets

Defrosting: Arrange with the thinnest parts towards the centre on a microwave rack over a plate. Cover with a plate, lid or greaseproof (waxed) paper.

If in a block, separate as soon as possible and arrange as before.

Quantity	Time on Medium-Low (all power outputs)
225 g/8 oz	3 mins
450 g/1 lb	5–6 mins

Standing time: 5 minutes, covered with a dome of foil, shiny side in.

Cooking: Arrange in a single layer in a shallow dish, thinnest parts overlapping towards the centre, or roll up. Brush with melted butter, or pour in a little milk, stock, wine or water, and add other flavourings of your choice. Cover with a lid, greaseproof (waxed) paper or clingfilm (plastic wrap), rolled back slightly at one edge.

Check thinner parts are not overcooking. If so, cover with a thin strip of foil to prevent further cooking.

Quantity	Time on Full Power			
	600–650w	700–750w	800–850w	900–1000w
225 g/8 oz	2–2½ mins	1½–2 mins	1½ mins	1–1½ mins
450 g/1 lb	3½–4 mins	3–3½ mins	2½–3 mins	2–2½ mins

Standing time: 2 minutes, covered with a dome of foil, shiny side in.

Whole sole

Defrosting: Place on a microwave rack over a plate. Cover with a plate, lid or greaseproof (waxed) paper.

Quantity	Time on Medium-Low (all power outputs)
1 fish, about 225 g/8 oz	3–4 mins
1 fish, about 450 g/1 lb	5–6 mins

Standing time: 5 minutes, covered with a dome of foil, shiny side in.

Cooking: Cook a maximum of two 225 g/8 oz fish or one larger one at a time. Place in a shallow dish. Brush with melted butter, or pour in a little milk, stock, wine or water, and add other flavourings of your choice. Protect the tails with a thin strip of foil. Cover with a lid, greaseproof (waxed) paper or clingfilm (plastic wrap), rolled back slightly at one edge.

Quantity	Time on Full Power			
	600–650w	700–750w	800–850w	900–1000w
225 g/8 oz	2–2½ mins	1½–2 mins	1½ mins	1–1½ mins
450 g/1 lb	4 mins	3½ mins	3 mins	2½–3 mins

Standing time: 5 minutes, covered with a dome of foil, shiny side in.

Swordfish or marlin steaks

Defrosting: Arrange on a microwave rack over a plate. Cover with a plate, lid or greaseproof (waxed) paper.

If in a block, separate as soon as possible and arrange around the rack.

Quantity	Time on Medium-Low (all power outputs)
225 g/8 oz	3 mins
450 g/1 lb	5–6 mins

Standing time: 5 minutes, covered with a dome of foil, shiny side in.

Cooking: Remove the dark skin around the steaks, if liked. Arrange in a single layer in a shallow dish. Brush with melted butter, or pour in a little stock, wine or water, and add other flavourings of your choice. Cover with a lid, greaseproof (waxed) paper or clingfilm (plastic wrap), rolled back slightly at one edge.

Quantity	Time on Full Power			
	600–650w	700 750w	800–850w	900–1000w
225 g/8 oz	2–2½ mins	1½–2 mins	1½ mins	1–1½ mins
450 g/1 lb	3½–4 mins	3–3½ mins	2½–3 mins	2–2½ mins

Standing time: 2 minutes, covered with a dome of foil, shiny side in.

Trout fillets

Defrosting: Arrange with the thinnest parts towards the centre on a microwave rack over a plate. Cover with a plate, lid or greaseproof (waxed) paper.

If in a block, separate as soon as possible and arrange as before.

Quantity	Time on Medium-Low (all power outputs)
225 g/8 oz	3 mins
450 g/1 lb	5–6 mins

Standing time: 5 minutes, covered with a dome of foil, shiny side in.

Cooking: Arrange in a single layer in a shallow dish, thinnest parts overlapping towards the centre. Brush with melted butter, or pour in a little stock, wine or water, and add other flavourings of your choice. Cover with a lid, greaseproof (waxed) paper or clingfilm (plastic wrap), rolled back slightly at one edge.

Check thinner parts are not overcooking. If so, cover with thin strips of foil to prevent further cooking.

Quantity	Time on Full Power			
	600–650w	700–750w	800–850w	900–1000w
225 g/8 oz	2–2½ mins	1½–2 mins	1½ mins	1–1½ mins
450 g/1 lb	3½–4 mins	3–3½ mins	2½–3 mins	2–2½ mins

Standing time: 2 minutes, covered with a dome of foil, shiny side in.

Whole trout

Defrosting: Place up to two at a time head to tail on a microwave rack over a plate. Cover with a plate, lid or greaseproof (waxed) paper.

Quantity	Time on Medium-Low (all power outputs)
1	3–4 mins
2	5–6 mins

Standing time: 5 minutes, covered with a dome of foil, shiny side in.

Cooking: Rinse and trim fins and tail. Make several slashes in each side of the body. Place head to tail in a shallow dish. Brush with melted butter, or pour in a little stock, wine or water, and add other flavourings of your choice. Lay a thin strip of foil over the tail ends to prevent overcooking. Cover with a lid, greaseproof (waxed) paper or clingfilm (plastic wrap), rolled back slightly at one edge. Alternatively, lay individually on a double thickness of greaseproof paper, flavour as before, wrap and cook.

Quantity	Time on Full Power			
	600–650w	700–750w	800–850w	900–1000w
1	4 mins	3½ mins	3 mins	2½–3 mins
2	5–6 mins	4–4½ mins	3½–4 mins	3–3½ mins

Standing time: 2 minutes, covered with a dome of foil, shiny side in.

Smoked trout fillets

Defrosting: Arrange with the thinnest parts towards the centre on a microwave rack over a plate. Cover with a plate, lid or greaseproof (waxed) paper.

If in a block, separate as soon as possible and arrange as before.

Quantity	Time on Medium-Low (all power outputs)
225 g/8 oz	3 mins
450 g/1 lb	5–6 mins

Standing time: 5 minutes, covered with a dome of foil, shiny side in.

Cooking: Hot-smoked, or cooked, ready-to-eat, smoked fillets need no further cooking. Cold-smoked (or raw-smoked) trout can be cooked as follows.

Arrange in a single layer in a shallow dish, thinnest parts overlapping towards the centre. Brush with melted butter. Cover with a lid, greaseproof (waxed) paper or clingfilm (plastic wrap), rolled back slightly at one edge.

Check thinner parts are not overcooking. If so, cover with thin strips of foil to prevent further cooking.

Quantity	Time on Full Power			
	600–650w	700–750w	800–850w	900–1000w
225 g/8 oz	2–2½ mins	1½–2 mins	1½ mins	1–1½ mins
450 g/1 lb	3½–4 mins	3–3½ mins	2½–3 mins	2–2½ mins

Standing time: 2 minutes, covered with a dome of foil, shiny side in.

Whole smoked trout

Defrosting: Place up to two at a time head to tail on a microwave rack over a plate. Cover with a plate, lid or greaseproof (waxed) paper.

Quantity	Time on Medium-Low (all power outputs)
1	3–4 mins
2	6–8 mins

Standing time: 5 minutes, covered with a dome of foil, shiny side in.

Cooking: Place head to tail in a shallow dish. Brush with melted butter. Cover tail ends with thin strips of foil to prevent overcooking. Cover with a lid, greaseproof (waxed) paper or clingfilm (plastic wrap), rolled back slightly at one edge.

Quantity	Time on Full Power			
	600–650w	700–750w	800–850w	900–1000w
1	4 mins	3½ mins	3 mins	2½–3 mins
2	5–6 mins	4–4½ mins	3½–4 mins	3–3½ mins

Standing time: 2 minutes, covered with a dome of foil, shiny side in.

Tuna steaks

Defrosting: Arrange with the thinnest parts towards the centre on a microwave rack over a plate. Cover with a plate, lid or greaseproof (waxed) paper.

If in a block, separate as soon as possible and arrange as before.

Quantity	Time on Medium-Low (all power outputs)
225 g/8 oz	3 mins
450 g/1 lb	5–6 mins

Standing time: 5 minutes, covered with a dome of foil, shiny side in.

Cooking: Arrange in a single layer in a shallow dish. Brush with melted butter, or pour in a little wine, stock or water, and add other flavourings of your choice. Cover with a lid, greaseproof (waxed) paper or clingfilm (plastic wrap), rolled back slightly at one edge.

If you like your tuna steaks pink in the middle, reduce the cooking time.

Quantity	Time on Full Power			
	600–650w	700–750w	800–850w	900–1000w
225 g/8 oz	2–2½ mins	1½–2 mins	1½ mins	1–1½ mins
450 g/1 lb	3½–4 mins	3–3½ mins	2½–3 mins	2–2½ mins

Standing time: 2 minutes, covered with a dome of foil, shiny side in.

Whiting

Defrosting: Arrange with the thinnest parts towards the centre on a microwave rack over a plate. Cover with a plate, lid or greaseproof (waxed) paper.

If in a block, separate as soon as possible and arrange as before.

Quantity	Time on Medium-Low (all power outputs)
225 g/8 oz	3 mins
450 g/1 lb	5–6 mins

Standing time: 5 minutes, covered with a dome of foil, shiny side in.

Cooking: Arrange in a single layer in a shallow dish, thinnest parts overlapping towards the centre. Brush with melted butter, or pour in a little milk, stock, wine or water, and add other flavourings of your choice. Cover with a lid, greaseproof (waxed) paper or clingfilm (plastic wrap), rolled back slightly at one edge.

Check thinner parts are not overcooking. If so, cover with a thin strip of foil to prevent further cooking.

Quantity	Time on Full Power			
	600–650w	700–750w	800–850w	900–1000w
225 g/8 oz	2–2½ mins	1½–2 mins	1½ mins	1–1½ mins
450 g/1 lb	3½–4 mins	3–3½ mins	2½–3 mins	2–2½ mins

Standing time: 2 minutes, covered with a dome of foil, shiny side in.

Meat

Many meats can be defrosted and cooked successfully in the microwave. However, tender cuts work much better than tough cuts that require long, slow cooking (best done conventionally or in a pressure cooker). Cooked meat dishes too can be defrosted and reheated beautifully.

Cooking meat

Minced (ground) meat
Minced meat cooks well in a microwave, either with or without a sauce. There is no need to add fat. Simply spread the meat in a thin layer in a shallow dish, cover and cook on Full Power, stirring every 30 seconds, until no longer pink and all the grains are separate. Pour the melted fat from the dish before adding sauce or vegetables.

Burgers
Meat, vegetable and quorn burgers cook well in the microwave. Ideally, use a browning dish (see pages 22–3) but they can be cooked on a microwave rack over a plate to catch the drips.

Chops and steaks
These are particularly good cooked on a browning dish. Alternatively, for chops, coat in a browning agent (see page 24) before cooking. For beef steaks, I recommend you grill (broil) or fry (sauté) them conventionally. Both chops and steaks can also be cooked in a sauce in a casserole dish (Dutch oven). Choose chops or steaks of equal size if you want to cook more than one at a time. Cook with the thickest edge of meat to the outside of the dish and make sure they do not overlap. Just cover them in sauce (a can of condensed soup, for instance) and add any flavourings like herbs, but no salt. Cook them on Full Power in their sauce until the liquid boils, then cook on Medium for 30 minutes per 450 g/1 lb meat. Taste and season before serving.

Offal

Liver and kidneys cook quickly and well in a microwave in a sauce. Make sure they are cut into even-sized pieces and take care not to overcook as the flesh toughens easily. Place in a casserole dish (Dutch oven), just cover with a sauce, cook on Full Power until the sauce bubbles, then cook on Medium until tender – test after every minute. Liver can also be cooked on a browning dish (see pages 22–3).

Hearts need long, slow cooking and are best cooked conventionally.

Sausages

It's only worth microwaving sausages if you have a browning dish (see pages 22–3). If not, I recommend that you cook them conventionally. You can defrost them, however. For a smoked pork ring and frankfurters, see the preparation and cooking times in Convenience foods on page 31.

Casseroles

Don't try and cook casseroles using tough cuts that require long, slow cooking; the result will be disappointing. But chicken and other poultry, game, tender cuts of meat, such as chops or steaks, and quorn steaks and pieces can be 'casseroled' in a sauce very successfully using the following method.

Cook any onion or vegetables in a little oil in a casserole dish (Dutch oven) for 1–2 minutes until slightly softened. Brown the meat conventionally in a frying pan (skillet), then add to the vegetables with the liquid and flavourings. Do not add salt until fully cooked.

For best results, follow these guidelines.

- Use no more than 300 ml/½ pt/1¼ cups liquid to each 450 g/ 1 lb meat.

- Make sure the dish is large enough to allow for the liquid bubbling up inside the covered dish but not so large the food sits in a thin layer or it will dry up as microwave cooking time is longer than normal.

- Cook on Full Power until the liquid boils, then turn down to Medium and cook for 30 minutes per 450 g/1 lb meat.

- Test, then cook in 3-minute bursts until cooked through.

- Lift out the meat, cover and leave to stand while you thicken the juices. Blend a little cornflour (cornstarch) with some cold water. Stir in, return to the microwave and cook on Full Power for 1–2 minutes until thickened. Stir again, taste and season as necessary. Return the meat to the casserole, microwave on Full Power for 1 minute to reheat, and serve.

- Quorn steaks and pieces are very tender and need only to be heated in the sauce for flavour. I recommend no more than 15 minutes per 450 g/1 lb.

Barbecues
Chops, sausages, poultry and game can all be cooked quickly in the microwave, then finished off on the barbecue. This ensures they are cooked through thoroughly.

Bacon and gammon
Bacon rashers (slices): These cook well in the microwave because the high percentage of fat to lean encourages browning and crisping.

- Always cook rashers on a microwave rack with a dish beneath to catch fat drips.

- Cover the bacon with a dome, an upturned bowl, greaseproof (waxed) paper or kitchen paper (paper towels) – but take care as kitchen paper tends to stick – to prevent splashes of fat.

- Cook on Full Power for 20 seconds to 1 minute per rasher, depending on the power output of your oven and the thickness and size of the rashers.

Gammon steaks and bacon chops: Cook on a microwave rack or use a browning dish (see pages 22–3). Always remove the rind from bacon and gammon and snip the fat and rind at intervals to stop the meat curling as it cooks.

Stuffed bacon rolls (Angels or devils on horseback): Make the rolls in the usual way and secure them with wooden cocktail sticks (toothpicks). Arrange them around the edge of a plate and cover as for bacon rashers (slices). Rearrange and turn over when they start to spit. Cook until the bacon is lightly browned but not hard.

Gammon and bacon joints: These keep their shape and flavour when cooked in the microwave and are especially good if you want to slice the meat and serve it cold. Unless the joint is one of the pre-shaped, round kind, it must be soaked overnight in two or three changes of water, otherwise salt will remain in the meat rather than dissolving as it does when boiled or cooked in a conventional oven and the result will be unbearably salty.

- Always cook gammon and bacon joints in a roasting bag. If you want to glaze the fat, remove the rind after cooking, cut the surface of the fat into diamond shapes, brush with warmed honey or marmalade and brown under a conventional grill (broiler).

Kebabs
Because kebabs are made with tender cuts of meat, fish, offal or poultry, they cook well in a microwave. Follow these general rules.

- Marinate meat or poultry first for added flavour and colour (see Browning foods, page 24).

- Use soaked wooden skewers, not metal ones, and cook up to four at one time.

- Cut foods into even-sized pieces for more even cooking.

- Place on a microwave rack over a plate to catch any juices, or use a browning dish (see pages 22–3).

- Cover with a dome of greaseproof (waxed) paper to prevent spluttering.

• Microwave on Full Power for 1–2 minutes per kebab, depending on the power output of your oven. Turn over. Continue cooking in 30-second bursts, until cooked to your liking (the exact time depends on the type and quantity of food), turning again, if necessary.

Pâtés and terrines

These cook much more quickly in a microwave. Prepare in your normal way. Turn into a suitable, microwave-safe container. Cover with greaseproof (waxed) paper. Cook on Medium-High for 20–30 minutes per 900 g/2 lb meat until the mixture feels just firm to the touch. Cover with clean greaseproof paper and weigh down with heavy weights. Leave until cold, then chill overnight.

Note: Pâtés and delicatessen meats to be served cold are not suitable for defrosting in the microwave. The fat will run and the food become warm before it is defrosted.

Defrosting meat

With a microwave, joints can be defrosted in under 2 hours, and most smaller cuts in under an hour. Unfortunately, you can't just put the meat in, turn the microwave to 'defrost' and leave it. The defrosting must be done in short bursts with standing time in between and the meat turned frequently, to make sure the thinner parts do not start to cook before the centre is defrosted. If your microwave has an auto-defrost facility, it will automatically stop the oven and tell you to turn the meat before restarting after the sufficient standing time. See the individual entries over the next few pages for details of correct timings.

Chops, steaks, sausages, offal, bacon, minced (ground) and cubed meat can be defrosted completely in the microwave, following the simple guidelines on page 82.

Joints are best started in the microwave, then left to complete defrosting at room temperature. Most joints are an uneven shape, and this makes uniform defrosting difficult, but the whole process can still take under 2 hours.

Small, thin pieces of meat can be defrosted and cooked in one operation, but results are not very good (with the exception of burgers). It is best, whenever possible, to defrost, then cook.

Standing times

Standing time is important for good results. During standing time, heat spreads through the food, defrosting the centre where microwaves cannot penetrate. Unless otherwise stated, always wrap food in foil, shiny side in, during standing time. This keeps the heat in and encourages defrosting.

If you have a microwave with automatic or 'cyclic' defrosting, it will pulse energy on and off during the selected defrosting time, so that standing time is built into the process. It is still a good idea to give some foil-wrapped standing time at the end of defrosting for even results.

Note: Extra microwaving will not reduce the standing time, so don't be tempted to try this. All that will happen is that the outside of the meat will begin to cook while the centre remains frozen.

Preparing meat for defrosting

Meat gives out liquid during defrosting, so a microwave rack is essential. Stand the microwave rack over a shallow dish so the liquid drips through. If you allow the meat to stand in the liquid, it will begin to cook as the liquid heats up.

Joints

- Leave the joint in the freezer wrapper. Put on the microwave rack over a shallow dish. After 15 minutes of defrosting, unwrap. If it has a bone, protect the ends with small, smooth pieces of foil.

- Stand the joint on the microwave rack and cover with a dome of greaseproof (waxed paper), clingfilm (plastic wrap) or an upturned dish that will cover the meat completely.

- If the joint is an uneven shape (such as a leg or shoulder), position with the thickest part towards the outside. If the joint is big and it isn't possible to do this, protect the thinnest end with a smooth piece of foil.

Sliced meat
Thick slices of meat (such as braising steak) often stick together when frozen, so start the meat defrosting in its pack. As soon as it has defrosted sufficiently, separate the pieces and arrange them on the microwave rack so that the thickest edges are towards the outside. Cover with clingfilm (plastic wrap), a dome or inverted dish that covers the meat completely and continue defrosting.

Cubed meat
If the meat has been freeflow frozen (i.e. isn't stuck together), arrange the cubes on a microwave rack and cover. As the meat defrosts, rearrange the pieces, moving the most frozen ones from the centre to the edge.

If the meat has been frozen in a solid block, put it on the microwave rack and cover. As the cubes defrost and can be separated from the block, remove and wrap them in foil to stand while the remainder defrost.

Sausages
If sausages are stuck together, start defrosting them in their pack, then free them as soon as possible. Arrange around the edge of a microwave rack to finish defrosting, covering with greaseproof (waxed) paper or clingfilm (plastic wrap).

Freeflow sausages (frozen separately) should be arranged in a circle around the edge of the microwave rack. Make an inner circle too, if necessary, then cover. Move the sausages around as they begin to defrost.

Bacon rashers (slices)
Start bacon rashers defrosting in their pack on a microwave rack over a plate. As soon as the top rasher is soft, open the pack and peel away as many rashers as you can. Wrap them in foil while the remainder defrost.

Continue defrosting on the microwave rack, peeling rashers away as soon as they become soft enough.

Minced (ground) meat and sausagemeat

If the meat is freeflow frozen, there is no need to defrost it before cooking.

Mince frozen in a block should be put on the microwave rack, then covered with a dome of greaseproof (waxed) paper, clingfilm (plastic wrap), or an inverted dish. As the edges begin to defrost (before they begin to turn grey as it begins to cook), scrape the meat away and set aside in a foil-covered bowl.

Break up the block as soon as possible. If this is not done, the outside will cook while the centre remains frozen.

Sausagemeat should be defrosted in the same way.

Cooked meat dishes

Frozen casseroles and other meat dishes containing a sauce can be reheated from frozen on Full Power, but for best results, defrost first and then reheat on Medium. Don't try to reheat meat pies from frozen or the pastry (paste) will be completely soggy.

If a casserole was frozen in a dish, it can be defrosted and reheated in the same dish. If it wasn't, you will have to transfer the meat to a suitable container.

As the casserole or meat dish in sauce begins to defrost, the edges will melt. Break up the block as this happens and stir, rearranging any large pieces of meat, so that the colder parts are pushed to the outer edges.

Roasting meat

Small pieces of meat, such as stuffed pork or lamb tenderloin, roast well in the microwave but, in my opinion, larger joints are not as good as when cooked conventionally. However, you will discover what suits you when you have experimented a little. The chart on page 84 gives you complete times for microwave cooking but to reduce cooking times substantially and save you fuel, I recommend, ideally, a combination of microwave and conventional oven (unless you have a combination cooker).

Weigh your joint and cook in the microwave for half its cooking time (calculated by weight), then transfer to a hot conventional oven for the remaining cooking time (by weight). So, for example, cook a 1.75 kg/4 lb leg of lamb in the microwave for 12–16 minutes, then transfer to the hot conventional oven for 40 minutes. This saves about an hour. (While the meat is microwaving, you can save even more time by putting your potatoes in the top of the oven to start roasting!)

If you have a 900–1000 watt cooker, you may find it best to roast meat on Medium instead of Medium-High. If you do this, use the cooking times given in individual entries for a 700–750 watt cooker.

Meat temperature chart

Type of meat	Remove from the microwave at	Temperature after standing	Approximate cooking time per 450 g/1 lb on Medium-High
Beef, rare	49°C/120°F	60°C/140°F	6–8 minutes
Beef, medium	60°C/140°F	71°C/160°F	8–10 minutes
Beef, well-done	71°C/160°F	77°C/170°F	10–12 minutes
Lamb, medium	66°C/150°F	77°C/170°F	7–9 minutes
Lamb, well-done	71°C/160°F	82°C/180°F	10–12 minutes
Pork, gammon and ham	82°C/180°F	88°C/190°F	8–12 minutes
Veal	66°C/150°F	77°C/170°F	6–10 minutes
Chicken	82°C/180°F	88°C/190°F	7–10 minutes
Turkey	79°C/175°F	90°C/195°F	8–11 minutes

General rules for meat

• Position meat with the thickest parts towards the outside. Protect thin parts and bone ends with thin strips of smooth foil.

• Defrost meat completely before cooking.

• Usually, if meat takes more than 15 minutes to cook, it will brown in the microwave because of the high fat content. However, it won't look as brown as when cooked conventionally, so use a browning agent (see page 24) or marinade or place in a roaster bag to assist the process. Alternatively, use a browning dish (see pages 22–3).

- When using a roaster bag, put the meat on a microwave rack or upturned saucer over a plate and make a small slit in the base of the bag so the juices drain on to the plate.

- Don't salt meat before cooking or it will toughen the surface.

- Never use a conventional meat thermometer in the microwave. Use a special microwave meat thermometer (see page 12).

- For kebabs, use soaked wooden skewers, not metal.

- Meat is best cooked from room temperature. If cooking straight from the fridge, add a further 1–2 minutes per 450 g/1 lb.

- To test whether roast meat is cooked, test it with a skewer. It should feel tender. For a more definitive result, use a microwave meat thermometer (see page 12) and cook according to the table opposite.

Defrosting and cooking times for meat

In the following pages I have listed different types of meat and how to defrost and cook them to perfection. I cannot stress enough that all times are approximate as every microwave oven is different and every piece of meat is a slightly different size and shape. Always use the shortest time, test the meat, then add on a little more time as necessary.

Remember, standing time is **crucial** for perfect results.

Bacon rashers (slices)

Defrosting: Place in their wrapper on a microwave rack over a plate.

As soon as the top rasher is softening, peel off as many rashers as possible. Turn over. Stop defrosting as soon as possible. The rashers can be cooked as soon as they are separated.

Quantity	Time on Medium-Low (all power outputs)
8	2 mins

Standing time: None.

Wrap rashers in foil as they are removed until all are defrosted.

Cooking: Lay rashers on a microwave rack over a plate.
Cover loosely with greaseproof (waxed) paper or kitchen paper (paper towels).

Quantity	Time on Full Power			
	600–650w	700–750w	800–850w	900–1000w
1	1 min	45 secs	30 secs	20 secs

Standing time: None.

Burgers (all types)

Meat, veggie and quorn burgers can all be treated in the same way.
Cook from frozen.

Cooking: Arrange in a circle on a microwave rack over a plate.
Cover with greaseproof (waxed) paper to prevent spluttering.
Turn over halfway through cooking.

For quorn and veggie burgers, brush with a little oil before cooking.

Quantity	Time on Full Power			
	600–650w	700–750w	800–850w	900–1000w
1	1½ mins	1¼ mins	1 min	50 secs–1 min
2	3 mins	2½ mins	2 mins	1¾–3 mins
4	5–6 mins	4–6 mins	3½–4 mins	2½–3½ mins

Beef joint on the bone

Defrosting: Place on a microwave rack over a shallow dish to catch the drips. Cover with a dome of greaseproof (waxed) paper, clingfilm (plastic wrap) or an inverted dish.

Turn over every 5 minutes. Note standing time halfway through.

Quantity	Time on Medium-Low (all power outputs)
per 450 g/1 lb	5–8 mins

Standing time: 30 minutes, halfway through defrosting, wrapped in foil, shiny side in (remove before returning to the microwave).
After completing microwave defrosting time, re-wrap in foil and leave to finish defrosting at room temperature.

Cooking: Place on a microwave rack over a plate or shallow dish. Protect any bone ends with thin strips of foil, place in a roaster bag and seal with a plastic tie.

Turn the meat over halfway through cooking.

Quantity	Time on Medium–High			
	600–650w	700–750w	800–850w	900–1000w
per 450 g/1 lb				
Rare	5–6 mins	4½–5 mins	4–4½ mins	3½–4 mins
Medium	7–8 mins	6½–7 mins	6–6½ mins	5½–6 mins
Well-done	11–12 mins	10–11 mins	9–10 mins	8–9 mins

Standing time: 15–20 minutes for rare or medium, 20–25 minutes for well-done, covered with a dome of foil, shiny side in.

Beef joint without bone

This is suitable for boned and rolled joints, or boneless joints, like topside.

Defrosting: Place on a microwave rack over a shallow dish to catch the drips. Cover with a dome of greaseproof (waxed) paper, clingfilm (plastic wrap) or an inverted dish.

Turn over every 5 minutes. Note standing time halfway through.

Quantity	Time on Medium-Low (all power outputs)
per 450 g/1 lb	8–10 mins

Standing time: 30 minutes halfway through defrosting, wrapped in foil, shiny side in (remove before continuing microwaving).

After completing microwave defrosting time, re-wrap in foil and leave to finish defrosting at room temperature.

Cooking: Place on a microwave rack over plate or shallow dish, fat side down, place in a roaster bag and seal with a plastic tie.

Turn the meat over halfway through cooking.

Quantity	Time on Medium-High			
	600–650w	700–750w	800–850w	900–1000w
per 450 g/1 lb				
Rare	6–7 mins	5–6 mins	4–5 mins	3½–4 mins
Medium	9–10 mins	8–9 mins	7–8 mins	6–7 mins
Well-done	10–12 mins	9–10 mins	8–9 mins	7–8 mins

Standing time: 15–20 minutes for rare and medium, 20–25 minutes for well-done, covered with a dome of foil, shiny side in.

Beef steaks

Defrosting: Place on a microwave rack over a shallow dish to catch the drips, thickest parts facing outwards. Cover with a dome of greaseproof (waxed) paper, clingfilm (plastic wrap) or an inverted dish.

If in a solid block, begin to defrost in the wrapper, separate and arrange as soon as possible.

Turn over two or three times during defrosting.

Quantity	Time on Medium-Low (all power outputs)
per 450 g/1 lb	6–10 mins (depending on thickness)

Standing time: 5–10 minutes, wrapped in foil, shiny side in.

Cooking: I recommend cooking steaks in the microwave only if you use a browning dish (see page 22) or cook them in a sauce (see page 76).

Gammon and ham joints

Defrosting: Place on a microwave rack over a shallow dish to catch the drips. Cover with a dome of greaseproof (waxed) paper, clingfilm (plastic wrap) or an inverted dish.

Turn over every 5 minutes. Note standing time halfway through.

Quantity	Time on Medium-Low (all power outputs)
per 450 g/1 lb	8–10 mins

Standing time: 30 minutes halfway through defrosting, wrapped in foil, shiny side in (remove the foil before continuing microwaving).

After completing microwave defrosting time, re-wrap in foil and leave to finish defrosting at room temperature.

Cooking: Place in a casserole dish (Dutch oven) and add 150 ml/¼ pt/⅔ cup cider, white wine or apple juice. Cover.

Quantity	Time on Medium-High			
	600–650w	700–750w	800–850w	900–1000w
per 450 g/1 lb	11–12 mins	10–11 mins	9–10 mins	8–9 mins

Standing time: 30 minutes, covered with a dome of foil.

Use the cooking stock to make a sauce.

Gammon or ham steaks

Defrosting: Arrange one or two at a time around a microwave rack over a plate. Cover with a dome of greaseproof (waxed) paper, clingfilm (plastic wrap) or an inverted dish.

Turn over several times during defrosting.

Quantity	Time on Medium-Low (all power outputs)
1	2–3 mins
2	4–6 mins

Standing time: 5 minutes, wrapped in foil.

Cooking: Use a browning dish (see pages 22–3) or place on a microwave rack over a plate. Snip the edges with scissors to prevent curling. Cover with a roaster bag.

Turn over once halfway through cooking.

Quantity	Time on Medium-High			
	600–650w	700–750w	800–850w	900–1000w
1	2–3 mins	1½–2 mins	1–1½ mins	1 min
2	4–6 mins	3–4 mins	2–3 mins	1½–2 mins

Standing time: 2 minutes, covered with foil.

Lamb joints on the bone

Defrosting: Place on a microwave rack over a shallow dish to catch the drips.

Leave in its freezer wrapper for the first 15 minutes' defrosting, then remove, cover with a dome of greaseproof (waxed) paper, clingfilm (plastic wrap) or an inverted dish and continue defrosting.

Turn over every 5 minutes. Note standing time halfway through.

Quantity	Time on Medium-Low (all power outputs)
per 450 g/1 lb	5–8 mins

Standing time: 30 minutes halfway through defrosting, wrapped in foil, shiny side in (remove the foil before continuing to microwave).

When microwave defrosting time is complete, re-wrap in foil and leave to finish defrosting at room temperature.

Cooking: Place on a microwave rack over a plate or shallow dish. Protect any bone ends with thin strips of foil and place the joint in a roaster bag. Seal with a plastic tie.

Turn the meat over halfway through cooking.

Quantity	Time on Medium-High			
	600–650w	700–750w	800–850w	900–1000w
per 450 g/1 lb				
Medium	7–8 mins	6½–7 mins	6–6½ mins	5½–6 mins
Well-done	11–12 mins	10–11 mins	9–10 mins	8–9 mins

Standing time: 20–25 minutes, covered with a dome of foil, shiny side in.

Boned lamb joints

Defrosting: Place on a microwave rack over a shallow dish to catch the drips. Cover with a dome of greaseproopf (waxed) paper, clingfilm (plastic wrap) or an inverted dish.

Turn over every 5 minutes. Note standing time halfway through.

Quantity	Time on Medium-Low (all power outputs)
per 450 g/1 lb	8–10 mins

Standing time: 30 minutes halfway through defrosting, wrapped in foil, shiny side in (remove the foil before continuing to microwave).

When microwave defrosting time is complete, re-wrap in foil and leave to finish defrosting at room temperature.

Cooking: Stuff, if liked, tie and weigh joint. Place on a microwave rack over a plate or shallow dish, place in a roaster bag and seal with a plastic tie.

Turn the meat over halfway through cooking.

Quantity	Time on Medium-High			
	600–650w	700–750w	800–850w	900–1000w
per 450 g/1 lb				
Medium	8–9 mins	7–8 mins	6½–7 mins	6–6½ mins
Well-done	11–12 mins	10½–11 mins	10–10½ mins	9½–10 mins

Standing time: 30 minutes, covered with a dome of foil, shiny side in.

Lamb chops

Defrosting: Place on a microwave rack over a shallow dish to catch the drips, thickest parts facing outwards. Cover with a dome of greaseproof (waxed) paper, clingfilm (plastic wrap) or an inverted dish.

If in a solid block, begin to defrost in the wrapper, then separate and arrange as soon as possible.

Defrosting time will vary according to the thickness of the chops.

Turn over several times during defrosting.

Quantity	Time on Medium-Low (all power outputs)
per 450 g/1 lb	6–10 mins

Standing time: 5–10 minutes, wrapped in foil, shiny side in.

Cooking: Add a browning agent (see pages 24–5). Arrange in a circle on a microwave rack over a plate or shallow dish, bones inwards. Cover with a roaster bag.

Turn over halfway through cooking.

Quantity	Time on Medium-High			
	600–650w	700–750w	800–850w	900–1000w
1	3–5 mins	2–4 mins	1½–3 mins	1–2 mins
2	4–6 mins	3–5 mins	2–4 mins	1½–3 mins
3	5–7 mins	4–6 mins	3–5 mins	2–4 mins
4	6–8 mins	5–7 mins	4–6 mins	3–5 mins

Standing time: 2 minutes, wrapped in foil, shiny side in.

Liver and kidneys

Defrosting: Arrange in a circle on a microwave rack over a shallow dish to catch the drips. Cover with a dome of greaseproof (waxed) paper, clingfilm (plastic wrap) or an inverted dish.

If in a solid block, begin to defrost in the wrapper, then separate and arrange as soon as possible.

Turn over several times during defrosting.

Quantity	Time on Medium-Low (all power outputs)
per 450 g/1 lb	6–8 mins

Standing time: 5 minutes, wrapped in foil, shiny side in.

Cooking: Best grilled (broiled) or fried (sautéed) conventionally or cooked in a sauce (see page 77). You can use a browning dish (see pages 22–3) for liver.

Pork joint on the bone

Defrosting: Place on a microwave rack over a shallow dish to catch the drips. Cover with a dome of greaseproof (waxed) paper, clingfilm (plastic wrap) or an inverted dish.

Turn over every 5 minutes. Note standing time halfway through.

Quantity	Time on Medium-Low (all power outputs)
per 450 g/1 lb	5–8 mins

Standing time: 30 minutes, halfway through defrosting, wrapped in foil (remove the foil before continuing to microwave).

When microwave defrosting time is complete, re-wrap in foil and leave to finish defrosting at room temperature.

Cooking: Score the rind, if there is any. Place the joint on a microwave rack, in a shallow dish, rind down. Place in a roaster bag.

Turn over halfway through cooking.

Quantity	Time on Medium-High			
	600–650w	700–750w	800–850w	900–1000w
per 450 g/1 lb	9–10 mins	8–9 mins	7–8 mins	6½–7 mins

Standing time: 30 minutes, wrapped in foil, shiny side in.

Remove the rind when cooking is complete.

To crisp crackling before serving, grill (broil) it or place on the microwave rack, cover with kitchen paper (paper towels) and microwave on Full Power, checking every 30 seconds, until the whole surface has bubbled up. Leave to cool and crisp.

Boned pork joint

Defrosting: Place on a microwave rack over a shallow dish to catch the drips. Cover with a dome of greaseproof (waxed) paper, clingfilm (plastic wrap) or an inverted dish.

Turn over every 5 minutes. Note standing time halfway through.

Quantity	Time on Medium-Low (all power outputs)
per 450 g/1 lb	8–10 mins

Standing time: 30 minutes, halfway through defrosting, wrapped in foil (remove the foil before continuing to microwave).

When microwave defrosting time is complete, re-wrap in foil and leave to finish defrosting at room temperature.

Cooking: Score the rind and stuff the joint, if liked, then tie and weigh. Stand rind-down on a microwave rack over a plate or shallow dish, place in a roaster bag and seal with a plastic tie.

Turn the meat over halfway through cooking.

Quantity	Time on Medium-High			
	600–650w	700–750w	800–850w	900–1000w
per 450 g/1 lb	10–12 mins	9–11 mins	8–10 mins	7–8 mins

Standing time: 30 minutes, wrapped in foil, shiny side in.

Remove the rind when cooking is complete.

To crisp crackling before serving, grill (broil) it or place on the microwave rack, cover with kitchen paper (paper towels) and microwave on Full Power, checking every 30 seconds, until the whole surface has bubbled up. Leave to cool and crisp.

Pork chops

Defrosting: Arrange on a microwave rack, bone ends inwards, over a shallow dish to catch the drips. Cover with a dome of greaseproof (waxed) paper, clingfilm (plastic wrap) or an inverted dish.

If in a solid block, start defrosting in the wrapper, then separate and arrange as soon as possible.

Turn over several times during defrosting.

Quantity	Time on Medium-Low (all power outputs)
per 450 g/1 lb	6–10 mins

Standing time: 5–10 minutes, wrapped in foil, shiny side in.

Cooking: Add a browning agent (see page 24).
Arrange in a circle on a microwave rack over a plate or shallow dish, bones inwards. Cover with a roaster bag.

Turn over halfway through cooking.

Quantity	Time on Medium-High			
	600–650w	700–750w	800–850w	900–1000w
1	3–5 mins	2–3 mins	1½–2 mins	1–1½ mins
2	4–6 mins	3–5 mins	2–4 mins	1½–3 mins
3	6–8 mins	5–7 mins	4–6 mins	3½–5 mins
4	9–10 mins	8–9 mins	7–8 mins	6–7 mins

Standing time: 2 minutes, covered in foil, shiny side in.

Veal joint on the bone

Defrosting: Place on a microwave rack over a shallow dish. Cover with a dome of greaseproof (waxed) paper or clingfilm (plastic wrap).

Turn over every 5 minutes. Note standing time halfway through.

Quantity	Time on Medium-Low (all power outputs)
per 450 g/1 lb	5–8 mins

Standing time: 30 minutes, halfway through defrosting, wrapped in foil (remove before continuing to microwave).

When microwave defrosting time is complete, re-wrap in foil and finish defrosting at room temperature.

Cooking: Place on a microwave rack over a plate or shallow dish. Protect any bone ends with thin strips of foil, place in a roaster bag and seal with a plastic tie.

Turn the meat over halfway through cooking.

Quantity	Time on Medium-High			
	600–650w	700–750w	800–850w	900–1000w
per 450 g/1 lb	8–9 mins	7–8 mins	6–7 mins	5½–6 mins

Standing time: 30 minutes, covered with a dome of foil, shiny side in.

Boned veal joint

Defrosting: Place on a microwave rack over a shallow dish to catch the drips. Cover with a dome of greaseproof (waxed) paper, clingfilm (plastic wrap) or an inverted dish.

Turn over every 5 minutes. Note standing time halfway through.

Quantity	Time on Medium-Low (all power outputs)
per 450 g/1 lb	8–10 mins

Standing time: 30 minutes, halfway through defrosting, wrapped in foil (remove before continuing to microwave).

When microwave defrosting time is complete, re-wrap in foil and leave to finish defrosting at room temperature.

Cooking: Stuff, if liked, tie and weigh the joint. Place on a microwave rack over a plate, place in a roaster bag and seal with a plastic tie.

Turn the meat over halfway through cooking.

Quantity	Time on Medium-High			
	600–650w	700–750w	800–850w	900–1000w
per 450 g/1 lb	9–10 mins	8–9 mins	7–8 mins	6½–7 mins

Standing time: 30 minutes, covered with a dome of foil, shiny side in.

Veal chops

Defrosting: Arrange on a microwave rack, bone ends inwards, over a shallow dish to catch the drips. Cover with a dome of greaseproof (waxed) paper, clingfilm (plastic wrap) or an inverted dish.

If in a solid block, begin to defrost in the wrapper, then separate and arrange as soon as possible.

Quantity	Time on Medium-Low (all power outputs)
per 450 g/1 lb	6–10 mins

Standing time: 5–10 minutes, wrapped in foil, shiny side in.

Cooking: Add a browning agent (see page 24). Arrange in a circle on a microwave rack over a plate or shallow dish, bone ends inwards. Place in a roaster bag.

Turn over halfway through cooking.

Quantity	Time on Medium-High			
	600–650w	700–750w	800–850w	900–1000w
1	3–5 mins	2–3 mins	1½–2 mins	1–1½ mins
2	4–6 mins	3–5 mins	2–4 mins	1½–3 mins
3	6–8 mins	5–7 mins	4–6 mins	3½–5 mins
4	9–10 mins	8–9 mins	7–8 mins	6–7 mins

Standing time: 2 minutes, covered in foil, shiny side in.

Defrosting and cooking times
for cooked meat dishes

If simply reheating chilled foods, ignore the defrosting times and just use the cooking times. You may need to add on a little extra time if cooking items straight from the fridge.

Note: When making a shepherd's pie, lasagne, moussaka, etc. to be frozen, it is a good idea to put the food in a microwave-safe container so that it can be defrosted and reheated in the same dish. These meals can be cooked from frozen. Cook on Medium, turning the dish once or twice to avoid hot and cold spots and, make sure the food is piping hot throughout. However, for best results, defrost, then cook for the times given in the following pages. When reheating straight from frozen, you will need to add on extra cooking time – up to half as much again.

Casseroles

Defrosting: Remove any foil wrapping or plastic bag and place in a casserole dish (Dutch oven). If in a plastic freezer container, start the defrosting in this.

Break up as soon as possible and transfer to a casserole dish.

Quantity	Time on Medium-Low (all power outputs)
1 portion	6–8 mins
Family-size	15–20 mins

Reheating: Turn into a casserole dish (Dutch oven). Cover.

Stir frequently to distribute the heat evenly.

Quantity	Time on Full Power			
	600–650w	700–750w	800–850w	900–1000w
1 portion	3–5 mins	2½–4 mins	2–3 mins	2½ mins
Family-size	10–12 mins	9–11 mins	8–10 mins	7–9 mins

Standing time: 2–3 minutes, covered with a dome of foil, shiny side in.

Stir and serve.

Shepherd's pie

Defrosting: Remove any foil wrapper.
Place in a dish if necessary.

Turn two or three times during defrosting.

Quantity	Time on Medium-Low (all power outputs)
1 portion	6–8 mins
Family-size	10–15 mins

Standing time: 10 minutes, covered with a dome of foil, shiny side in.

Reheating: If just defrosted, remove the foil, cover with
and return to the microwave.

Quantity	Time on Medium			
	600–650w	700–750w	800–850w	900–1000w
1 portion	4–6 mins	3½–5 mins	3–4½ mins	3–3½ mins
Family-size	17–20 mins	14–17 mins	12–14 mins	10–12 mins

Standing time: 5 minutes, covered with a dome of foil, shiny side in.

Lasagne

Defrosting: Remove any foil wrapper.
Place in a dish, if necessary.

Turn two or three times during defrosting.

Quantity	Time on Medium-Low (all power outputs)
1 portion	5–8 mins
Family-size	9–15 mins

Standing time: 10 minutes, wrapped in foil, shiny side in.

Reheating: Remove any foil and cover.

Quantity	Time on Medium			
	600–650w	700–750w	800–850w	900–1000w
1 portion	5–6 mins	4–5 mins	3½–4½ mins	3–4 mins
Family-size	17–20 mins	15–17 mins	12–15 mins	10–12 mins

Standing time: 5 minutes.

Moussaka

Defrosting: Remove any foil packaging and place
in a dish if necessary. Cover.

Turn two or three times during defrosting.

Quantity	Time on Medium-Low (all power outputs)
1 portion	5–8 mins
Family-size	9–15 mins

Standing time: 10 minutes, wrapped in foil, shiny side in.

Reheating: Remove any foil and cover.

Quantity	Time on Medium			
	600–650w	700–750w	800–850w	900–1000w
1 portion	5–6 mins	4–5 mins	3½–4½ mins	3–4 mins
Family-size	17–20 mins	15–17 mins	12–15 mins	10–12 mins

Standing time: 5 minutes.

Chilli con carne

Defrosting: Remove any foil wrapping or plastic bag
and place in a casserole dish (Dutch oven). If it is in a plastic freezer
container, start in this.

Break up as soon as possible and transfer to a casserole dish.
Stir frequently whilst defrosting.

Quantity	Time on Medium-Low (all power outputs)
1 portion	6–8 mins
Family-size	15–20 mins

Reheating: Turn into a casserole dish (Dutch oven) and cover.

Stir frequently to distribute the heat evenly.

Quantity	Time on Full Power			
	600–650w	700–750w	800–850w	900–1000w
1 portion	3–5 mins	2½–4 mins	2–3 mins	2½ mins
Family-size	10–12 mins	9–11 mins	8–10 mins	7–9 mins

Standing time: 2–3 minutes, covered with a dome of foil, shiny side in.

Stir before serving

Meat curry

Defrosting: Remove any foil wrapping or plastic bag and place in a casserole dish (Dutch oven). If in a plastic freezer container, start the defrosting whilst still in this.

Break up as soon as possible and transfer to a casserole dish.
Stir frequently.

Quantity	Time on Medium-Low (all power outputs)
1 portion	6–8 mins
Family-size	15–20 mins

Reheating: Turn the curry into a casserole dish (Dutch oven) and cover.
Stir frequently to distribute the heat evenly.

Quantity	Time on Full Power			
	600–650w	700–750w	800–850w	900–1000w
1 portion	3–5 mins	2½–4 mins	2–3 mins	2½ mins
Family-size	10–12 mins	9–11 mins	8–10 mins	7–9 mins

Standing time: 2–3 minutes, covered with a dome of foil, shiny side in.
Stir before serving.

Poultry and Game

Microwaved poultry and game remain moist and tender.

General rules for poultry and game

- Poultry must be thoroughly defrosted before cooking in the microwave. Poultry with a cold spot in the centre won't cook properly and any salmonella bacteria in the bird could multiply and cause severe food poisoning. **Do not try to defrost a large whole bird completely in the microwave.**

- When casseroling poultry or game, remove the skin before cooking for better flavour and texture.

- Whole birds should be trussed. Shield wing tips and bone ends with thin strips of smooth foil.

- Stuff the neck, never the body cavity, of any poultry or game.

- Never salt the skin before cooking. It will draw out the moisture and toughen the flesh.

- Always give larger birds extra standing time halfway through cooking.

- When cooking any bird over 1.5 kg/3 lb in weight, start by cooking with the breast down. Turn over halfway through.

- I don't recommend cooking a whole goose in the microwave. It is too large and fatty to be microwaved successfully.

- Rabbit casseroles benefit from being left overnight, then reheated to enhance the flavour.

- Hare tends to be rather tough when cooked in the microwave and must be marinated first (see page 24).

- When roasting birds, use a browning agent (see page 24). Paprika and soy sauce are particularly good.

- Whole birds are best cooked in a roaster bag. However, you can put them in a casserole dish (Dutch oven) with a lid instead.

Defrosting poultry

As I have already stated, it is not advisable to defrost large whole birds completely in the microwave. Start the process in the microwave, then finish defrosting at room temperature. For best results, follow these general rules.

* Always check the bird is completely defrosted before starting to cook. The giblets should come away easily from the body cavity and no ice crystals should remain.

* As a guide, allow 2 minutes per 450 g/1 lb on Medium-Low, then leave to stand. The whole process will take 2–4 hours, compared with 8–12 if left at room temperature.

  Note: In an emergency, you can defrost completely in the microwave if cooking straight away. Defrost on Low (not Medium-Low) for 10–20 minutes per 450 g/1 lb. Shield wing tips, legs and parson's nose with thin strips of foil and turn the bird frequently during defrosting. Leave to stand for 1 hour after microwaving before starting to cook the bird.

* Portions may be defrosted completely. Place on a microwave rack, cover with kitchen paper (paper towels) and defrost on Medium-Low for 5–6 minutes per 450 g/1 lb, turning frequently. Wrap portions individually in foil after microwaving and leave to stand for 15 minutes before cooking.

Cooked poultry and game dishes

Frozen casseroles and other dishes containing game and poultry in a sauce can be reheated from frozen on Full Power, but for best results, defrost first and then reheat on Medium. If the food was frozen in a dish, it can be defrosted and reheated as it stands. If not, you will have to transfer it to a suitable container.

As the food begins to defrost, the edges will melt. Break up the block as this happens and stir, rearranging any large pieces of meat so that the colder parts are pushed to the outer edges.

Don't try to reheat poultry or game pies from frozen – the pastry (paste) will be completely soggy.

Cooked chicken joints or even tandoori chicken can also be reheated perfectly. I find it best to put them in a roaster bag over a microwave rack but you can put them in a casserole dish (Dutch oven) with a lid. Make sure you arrange them with the thinnest parts towards the centre.

Note: Pâtés and terrines made with poultry and game are not suitable for defrosting in the microwave. The fat will run and the food become warm before it has defrosted.

Defrosting and cooking times for poultry and game

Once again, remember that all times are approximate as every microwave oven is different and every piece of poultry is a slightly different size, shape and weight. Always use the shortest time, test to see if it is ready, then add on a little more time as necessary.

Remember, standing time is **crucial** for perfect results.

Whole chicken

Only small whole birds should be defrosted completely in the microwave. Ideally, partially defrost, then leave to complete defrosting at room temperature (see page 103).

Defrosting: Place the bird in its wrapper on a microwave rack over a plate. Check during defrosting and cover wing tips and leg bone ends with thin strips of foil to prevent cooking.

Note the power output in this case is Low (10 per cent). Turn over two or three times during defrosting.

Quantity	Time on Low (all power outputs)
per 450 g/1 lb	10–20 mins

Standing time: Up to 1 hour, covered with a dome of foil, shiny side in. Check that it has fully defrosted (see page 103) before cooking.

Cooking: Stuff the neck end, if liked, or put half an onion or some herbs in the body cavity. Truss, if necessary. Rub the skin with paprika or other browning agent (see page 24). Place breast down on a microwave rack over a plate or shallow dish. Place in a roaster bag and seal with a plastic tie.

Turn the bird over halfway through cooking.

Quantity	Time on Medium-High			
	600–650w	700–750w	800–850w	900–1000w
per 450 g/1 lb	8 mins	6–7 mins	5–6 mins	5 mins

Standing time: 30 minutes, covered with a dome of foil, shiny side in.

Chicken portions

Defrosting: Arrange on a microwave rack over a plate. Cover wing tips and leg bone ends with thin strips of foil to prevent cooking.

Turn over several times during defrosting.

Quantity	Time on Medium-Low (all power outputs)
per 450 g/1 lb	6 mins

Standing time: 30 minutes, covered with a dome of foil, shiny side in.

Cooking: Rub the skin with paprika or other browning agent (see page 24). Protect leg ends or wing tips with thin strips of foil to prevent overcooking. Place in a single layer on a microwave rack over a plate or shallow dish. Place in a roaster bag and seal with a plastic tie.

Turn over halfway through cooking.

Quantity	Time on Medium-High			
	600–650w	700–750w	800–850w	900–1000w
per 450 g/1 lb	8 mins	6–7 mins	5–6 mins	5 mins

Standing time: 5 minutes, wrapped in foil, shiny side in.

Chicken breast fillets

Defrosting: Arrange on a microwave rack over a plate.

Turn over several times during defrosting.

Quantity	Time on Medium-Low (all power outputs)
per 450 g/1 lb	5 mins

Standing time: 30 minutes, covered with a dome of foil, shiny side in.

Cooking: Rub with paprika or other browning agent (see page 24).
Place breast-down on a microwave rack over a plate or shallow dish.
Place in a roaster bag and seal with a plastic tie.

Turn over halfway through cooking.

Quantity	Time on Medium-High			
	600–650w	700–750w	800–850w	900–1000w
per 450 g/1 lb	8 mins	6–7 mins	5–6 mins	5 mins

Standing time: 5 minutes, wrapped in foil, shiny side in.

Whole capon

Don't attempt to defrost completely. Partially defrost using the time below,
then leave to finish defrosting at room temperature.

Defrosting: Place in its wrapper on a microwave rack over a plate.
Check during defrosting and cover wing tips and leg bone ends with
thin strips of foil if they start to cook.

Turn over several times during defrosting.

Quantity	Time on Medium-Low (all power outputs)
per 450 g/1 lb	2 mins

Standing time: 2–4 hours, covered with a dome of foil, shiny side in.
Check that it is completely defrosted (see page 103) before cooking.

Cooking: Stuff the neck end, if liked, or put half an onion or some herbs in the body cavity. Truss, if necessary. Rub the skin with paprika or other browning agent (see page 24). Place breast down on a microwave rack over a plate or shallow dish. Place in a roaster bag and seal with a plastic tie.

Turn the bird over halfway through cooking and leave to stand for 30 minutes, then continue cooking.

Quantity	Time on Medium-High			
	600–650w	700–750w	800–850w	900–1000w
per 450 g/1 lb	8 mins	6–7 mins	5–6 mins	5 mins

Standing time: 30 minutes, covered with a dome of foil, shiny side in. This is in addition to the standing time halfway through cooking (see above).

Whole duck

Don't attempt to defrost completely. Partially defrost using the time below, then leave to defrost completely at room temperature.

Defrosting: Place in its wrapper on a microwave rack over a plate.

Check during defrosting and cover wing tips and leg bone ends with thin strips of foil if they start to cook. Turn over several times during defrosting.

Quantity	Time on Medium-Low (all power outputs)
per 450 g/1 lb	2 mins

Standing time: 2–4 hours, covered with a dome of foil, shiny side in.

Check that it has completely defrosted (see page 103) before cooking.

Cooking: Stuff the neck end, if liked, or put half an onion or orange or some herbs in the body cavity. Truss, if necessary. Prick the skin all over with a fork. Rub the skin with paprika or other browning agent (see page 24). Place breast down on a microwave rack over a plate or shallow dish. Place in a roaster bag and seal with a plastic tie.

Turn the bird over halfway through cooking.

Quantity	Time on Medium-High			
	600–650w	700–750w	800–850w	900–1000w
per 450 g/1 lb	9 mins	8 mins	7 mins	6–7 mins

Standing time: 30 minutes, covered with a dome of foil, shiny side in.

Before serving, crisp the skin, if liked, under a preheated grill (broiler).

Duck or goose portions

Defrosting: Arrange on a microwave rack over a plate. Cover wing tips and leg bone ends with thin strips of foil to prevent cooking.

Turn over several times during defrosting.

Quantity	Time on Medium-Low (all power outputs)
per 450 g/1 lb	6 mins

Standing time: 30 minutes, covered with a dome of foil, shiny side in.

Cooking: Rub the skin with paprika or other browning agent (see page 24). Prick the skin with a fork. Place on a microwave rack over a plate or shallow dish. Cover wing tips and leg ends with thin strips of foil to prevent overcooking. Place in a roaster bag and seal with a plastic tie.

Turn over halfway through cooking.

Quantity	Time on Medium-High			
	600–650w	700–750w	800–850w	900–1000w
per 450 g/1 lb	9 mins	8 mins	7 mins	6–7 mins

Standing time: 5 minutes, wrapped individually in foil.

Before serving, crisp the skin under a preheated grill (broiler), if liked.

Grouse

Defrosting: Place in its wrapper on a microwave rack over a plate. Check during defrosting and cover wing tips and leg bone ends with thin strips of foil to prevent cooking.

Turn over several times during defrosting.

Quantity	Time on Medium-Low (all power outputs)
per 450 g/1 lb	6 mins

Standing time: Up to 1 hour, covered with a dome of foil, shiny side in.

Cooking: Put half an onion studded with a clove in the body cavity. Truss, if necessary. Rub the skin with paprika or another browning agent (see page 24). Place breast down on a microwave rack over a plate or shallow dish. Place in a roaster bag and seal with a plastic tie.

Turn the bird over halfway through cooking.

Quantity	Time on Medium			
	600–650w	700–750w	800–850w	900–1000w
per 450 g/1 lb	10 mins	9 mins	8 mins	7–8 mins

Standing time: 15 minutes, covered with a dome of foil, shiny side in.

Guinea fowl

Defrosting: Place in its wrapper on a microwave rack over a plate. Check during defrosting and cover wing tips and leg bone ends with thin strips of foil to prevent cooking.

Turn over several times during defrosting.

Quantity	Time on Medium-Low (all power outputs)
per 450 g/1 lb	6 mins

Standing time: Up to 1 hour, covered with a dome of foil, shiny side in.

Cooking: Put a slice of lemon, half an onion or some herbs in the body cavity. Truss, if necessary. Rub the skin with paprika or another browning agent (see page 24). Place breast down on a microwave rack over a plate or shallow dish. Place in a roaster bag and seal with a plastic tie.

Turn the bird over halfway through cooking.

Quantity	Time on Medium			
	600–650w	700–750w	800–850w	900–1000w
per 450 g/1 lb	10 mins	9 mins	8 mins	7–8 mins

Standing time: 15 minutes, covered with a dome of foil, shiny side in.

Partridge

Defrosting: Place in its wrapper on a microwave rack over a plate. Check during defrosting and cover wing tips and leg bone ends with thin strips of foil to prevent cooking.

Turn over several times during defrosting.

Quantity	Time on Medium-Low (all power outputs)
per 450 g/1 lb	6 mins

Standing time: Up to 1 hour, covered with a dome of foil, shiny side in.

Cooking: Put half an onion and a slice of orange in the body cavity. Truss, if necessary. Rub the skin with paprika or another browning agent (see page 24). Place breast down on a microwave rack over a plate or shallow dish. Place in a roaster bag and seal with a plastic tie.

Turn the bird over halfway through cooking.

Quantity	Time on Medium			
	600–650w	700–750w	800–850w	900–1000w
per 450 g/1 lb	12 mins	10 mins	8½ mins	8–8½ mins

Standing time: 15 minutes, covered with a dome of foil, shiny side in.

Pigeon

Defrosting: Place in its wrapper on a microwave rack over a plate. Check during defrosting and cover wing tips and leg bone ends with thin strips of foil to prevent cooking.

Turn over several times during defrosting.

Quantity	Time on Medium-Low (all power outputs)
per 450 g/1 lb	6 mins

Standing time: Up to 1 hour, covered with a dome of foil, shiny side in.

Cooking: Marinate in a red wine marinade, then casserole in the marinade. Cook up to four at a time.

Quantity	Time on Medium			
	600–650w	700–750w	800–850w	900–1000w
per pair	15 mins	13½ mins	12 mins	11–12 mins

Standing time: 5 minutes, covered with a dome of foil, shiny side in.

Poussin

Defrosting: Place in its wrapper on a microwave rack over a plate. Check during defrosting and cover wing tips and leg bone ends with thin strips of foil to prevent cooking.

Turn over several times during defrosting.

Quantity	Time on Medium-Low (all power outputs)
per 450 g/1 lb	6 mins

Standing time: Up to 1 hour, covered with a dome of foil, shiny side in.

Cooking: Leave whole or spatchcock (split down the backbone and open out flat). Cook up to four at a time. Rub the skin with paprika or another browning agent (see page 24). Place breast down on a microwave rack over a plate. Place in a roaster bag and seal with a plastic tie.

Turn over halfway through cooking.

Quantity	Time on Medium-High			
	600–650w	700–750w	800–850w	900–1000w
per 450 g/1 lb	8 mins	6½ mins	5 mins	4½–5 mins

Standing time: 15 minutes, covered with a dome of foil, shiny side in.

Whole turkey

Microwaving is not suitable for birds over 4.5 kg/10 lb. Don't attempt to defrost a whole bird completely. Partially defrost using the time below, then leave to defrost at room temperature.

Defrosting: Place in its wrapper on a microwave rack over a plate. Check during defrosting and cover wing tips and leg bone ends with thin strips of foil to prevent cooking.

Turn over several times during defrosting.

Quantity	Time on Medium-Low (all power outputs)
per 450 g/1 lb	2 mins

Standing time: 2–4 hours, covered with a dome of foil, shiny side in. Check that it has completely defrosted (see page 103) before cooking.

Cooking: Stuff the neck end, if liked, or put half an onion or some herbs in the body cavity. Truss, if necessary. Rub the skin with paprika or another browning agent (see page 24). Place breast down on a microwave rack over a plate. Place in a roaster bag and seal with a plastic tie.

Turn the bird over halfway through cooking and leave to stand for 30 minutes, then continue cooking.

Quantity	Time on Medium-High			
	600–650w	700–750w	800–850w	900–1000w
per 450 g/1 lb	8 mins	6–7 mins	5–6 mins	5 mins

Standing time: 30 minutes, covered with a dome of foil, shiny side in. This is in addition to the standing time halfway through (see above).

Turkey breast steaks

Defrosting: Arrange on a microwave rack over a plate.

Turn over several times during defrosting.

Quantity	Time on Medium-Low (all power outputs)
per 450 g/1 lb	5 mins

Standing time: 30 minutes, covered with a dome of foil, shiny side in.

Cooking: Rub with paprika or another browning agent
(see page 24). Place breast down on a microwave rack over a plate or
shallow dish. Place in a roaster bag and seal with a plastic tie.

Turn over halfway through cooking.

Quantity	Time on Medium-High			
	600–650w	700–750w	800–850w	900–1000w
per 450 g/1 lb	8 mins	6–7 mins	5–6 mins	5 mins

Standing time: 5 minutes, wrapped individually in foil, shiny side in.

Boneless turkey roast

Defrosting: Place on a microwave rack over a plate.

Turn over several times during defrosting.

Quantity	Time on Medium-Low (all power outputs)
per 450 g/1 lb	6 mins

Standing time: 30 minutes, covered with a dome of foil, shiny side in.

Cooking: Rub with paprika or another browning agent (see page 24).
Place on a microwave rack over a plate or shallow dish.
Place in a roaster bag and seal with a plastic tie.

Turn over halfway through cooking.

Quantity	Time on Medium-High			
	600–650w	700–750w	800–850w	900–1000w
per 450 g/1 lb	8 mins	6–7 mins	5–6 mins	5 mins

Standing time: 20 minutes, wrapped individually in foil, shiny side in.

Chicken or game casseroles

Defrosting: Remove any foil wrapping or plastic bag
and place in a casserole dish (Dutch oven). If it was frozen in a plastic
freezer container, start in this.

Break up as soon as possible and transfer to a casserole dish.
Stir frequently whilst defrosting.

Quantity	Time on Medium-Low (all power outputs)
1 portion	6–8 mins
Family-size	15–20 mins

Reheating: Turn into a casserole dish (Dutch oven). Cover.

Stir frequently to distribute the heat evenly.

Quantity	Time on Full Power			
	600–650w	700–750w	800–850w	900–1000w
1 portion	3–5 mins	2½–4 mins	2–3 mins	2½ mins
Family-size	10–12 mins	9–11 mins	8–10 mins	7–9 mins

Standing time: 2–3 minutes, covered with a dome of foil, shiny side in.

Stir before serving.

Chicken curry

Defrosting: Remove any foil wrapping or plastic bag and place in a casserole dish (Dutch oven). If it was frozen in a plastic freezer container, start in this.

Break up as soon as possible, taking care not to damage any chicken joints, and transfer to a casserole dish. Stir frequently whilst defrosting.

Quantity	Time on Medium-Low (all power outputs)
1 portion	6–8 mins
Family-size	15–20 mins

Reheating: Turn the curry into a casserole dish and cover.

Stir frequently to distribute the heat evenly, moving the chicken joints around so the thickest parts are towards the outside of the dish.

Quantity	Time on Full Power			
	600–650w	700–750w	800–850w	900–1000w
1 portion	3–5 mins	2½–4 mins	2–3 mins	2½ mins
Family-size	10–12 mins	9–11 mins	8–10 mins	7–9 mins

Standing time: 2–3 minutes, covered with a dome of foil, shiny side in.

Stir before serving.

Tandoori chicken

This may be reheated from frozen.

Reheating: Unwrap and place in a casserole dish (Dutch oven).

Break up the pieces as soon as possible and arrange, with the thinnest parts to the centre, on a microwave rack in a roaster bag. Tie with a plastic tie.

Rearrange twice during cooking.

Quantity	Time on Full Power			
	600–650w	700–750w	800–850w	900–1000w
2 portions	7 mins	6 mins	5 mins	4½ mins
4 portions	11 mins	9½ mins	8 mins	7½ mins

Standing time: 5 minutes, wrapped tightly in foil, shiny side in.

Roast chicken portions

These can be reheated from frozen.

Reheating: Unwrap and arrange with the thinnest parts to the centre on a microwave rack in a roaster bag. Tie with a plastic tie. Alternatively, arrange in a casserole dish (Dutch oven) and cover.

Rearrange twice during cooking.

Quantity	Time on Full Power			
	600–650w	700–750w	800–850w	900–1000w
2 portions	7 mins	6 mins	5 mins	4½ mins
4 portions	11 mins	9½ mins	8 mins	7½ mins

Standing time: 5 minutes, wrapped tightly in foil, shiny side in.

Peking duck

This can be reheated from frozen.

Reheating: Remove any wrapping and if the skin is already loose, remove it. Place on a microwave rack in a roaster bag and tie with a plastic tie. Alternatively, place in a casserole dish (Dutch oven) and cover.

Rearrange twice during cooking.

Quantity	Time on Full Power			
	600–650w	700–750w	800–850w	900–1000w
2 portions	7 mins	6 mins	5 mins	4½ mins
1 whole duck	12 mins	10 mins	9 mins	8½ mins

Standing time: 5 minutes, wrapped tightly in foil, shiny side in.

Grill (broil) the skin that you removed earlier until crisp before serving.

Pasta, Rice and Other Grains

Pasta, rice and other grains all cook very well in the microwave. Rice grains don't stick together; pasta is tender but still *al dente* and the kitchen remains free from steam. Also, if you use a large enough container, they are far less likely to boil over. However, none of them cooks much more quickly in the microwave than when cooked conventionally. Use the cooking time on the packet as a guide and check frequently during cooking as brands do vary.

General rules for pasta, rice and grains

Bulghar (cracked wheat)
Bulghar tastes much better if lightly toasted first. This can be done in the microwave before cooking in water (see page 118), but you can omit this if you prefer. To turn cooked bulghar into Tabbouleh, simply add chopped garlic, fresh mint and fresh parsley to taste and some chopped cucumber and tomatoes, if liked. Moisten with olive oil and lemon juice and season to taste.

Couscous
Couscous cooks beautifully and remains fluffy. Don't try to cook more than 225 g/8 oz at one time.

Pasta – all types
- Unlike other foods, the quantity of pasta does not affect the cooking time so much. More than the quantity suggested here may take a little longer, less will need much the same time.

- Don't try and cook more than 450 g/1 lb pasta in one go – 225 g/8 oz is ideal. Larger quantities would need far too large a container to fit comfortably in your microwave.

- Wholewheat varieties take slightly longer to cook.

- Always remove from the microwave when it still has some 'bite' or it will go soggy.

- Never leave to stand for longer than stated, for the same reason.

- If using quick-cook pasta, cook for the time stated on the packet, but check frequently to prevent overcooking.

Polenta
Only the precooked, 'instant' polenta is really successful in the microwave. Don't try to cook more than 225 g/8 oz/1⅓ cups at one time or it will go lumpy.

Rice
Like pasta, rice needs a large container so it can boil without bubbling over. Don't try to cook more than 350 g/12 oz/1½ cups in one go. It is best cooked in a measured amount of water, all of which is absorbed during cooking. The cooking time will be much the same regardless of quantity.

To reheat pasta or rice
Place in a dish. Add 15–30 ml water and cover. Microwave on Full Power, stirring every minute, until piping hot.

Cooking times for pasta, rice and other grains

Bulghar (cracked wheat)

Cooking: Place the bulghar in a large dish and microwave on Full Power for 2–3 minutes until lightly toasted, stirring once. Add boiling water (600 ml/1 pt/2½ cups for the quantity of bulghar given below – adjust for smaller quantities) and stir well.

Quantity	Time on Full Power			
	600–650w	700–750w	800–850w	900–1000w
225 g/8 oz/ 2 cups	5 mins	4½ mins	4 mins	3½–4 mins

Standing time: 2 minutes, covered with a dome of foil, shiny side in. The liquid should now be absorbed.

Season to taste and fluff up with a fork.

Couscous

Cooking: Put 600 ml/1 pt/2½ cups water and a chicken or vegetable stock cube in a large bowl (adjust the quantity of water if you are cooking less couscous than I have given here). Microwave on Full Power until boiling. Stir to dissolve the cube. Add the couscous and 30 ml/2 tbsp olive oil. Stir well.

Quantity	Time on Full Power			
	600–650w	700–750w	800–850w	900–1000w
225 g/8 oz/ 1⅓ cups	5 mins	4 mins	3 mins	2–3 mins

Standing time: 5 minutes, covered with a dome of foil, shiny side in. The liquid should now be absorbed.

Season to taste and fluff up with a fork.

Fresh pasta

Cooking: Place in a large dish. Cover with plenty of boiling water and add a pinch of salt. Stir well.

Check frequently and remove when the pasta still has some 'bite'.

Quantity	Time on Full Power			
	600–650w	700–750w	800–850w	900–1000w
225 g/8 oz	2–3 mins	2–2½ mins	1½–2 mins	1–1½ mins

Standing time: 2 minutes, covered with a dome of foil, shiny side in.

Drain and use immediately.

Macaroni and other pasta shapes

Cooking: Place in a large dish. Cover with plenty of boiling water and add a pinch of salt. Stir well.

Check frequently, stir once or twice and remove when the pasta still has some 'bite'.

Quantity	Time on Full Power			
	600–650w	700–750w	800–850w	900–1000w
225 g/8 oz	10 mins	9–10 mins	8–9 mins	8 mins

Standing time: 5 minutes, covered with a dome of foil, shiny side in.

Drain and use immediately.

Polenta

Cooking: Place in a large dish. Stir in 1.2 litres/2 pts/ 5 cups boiling water, chicken or vegetable stock (adjust the quantity for smaller amounts of polenta). Stir well.

Stir every 2 minutes during cooking until thick and the mixture leaves the sides of the dish.

Quantity	Time on Full Power			
	600–650w	700–750w	800–850w	900–1000w
225 g/8 oz/ 1⅓ cups	9 mins	8 mins	7 mins	6½–7 mins

Standing time: 1 minute, covered with a dome of foil, shiny side in.

Beat in 25 g/1 oz/2 tbsp butter and season with salt and pepper. Sprinkle liberally with grated Parmesan cheese and chopped fresh parsley before serving.

Ribbon noodles and tagliatelle

Cooking: Place in a large dish. Cover with plenty of boiling water and add a pinch of salt. Stir well.

Check frequently, stir once or twice and remove when the pasta still has some 'bite'.

Quantity	Time on Full Power			
	600–650w	700–750w	800–850w	900–1000w
225 g/8 oz	9–10 mins	8–9 mins	8 mins	8 mins

Standing time: 5 minutes, covered with a dome of foil, shiny side in.

Drain and use immediately.

Spaghetti

Cooking: Place in a large dish. Cover with plenty of boiling water and add a pinch of salt. Stir well.

Check frequently, stir once or twice and remove when the pasta still has some 'bite'.

Quantity	Time on Full Power			
	600–650w	700–750w	800–850w	900–1000w
225 g/8 oz	9–10 mins	8–9 mins	8 mins	8 mins

Standing time: 5 minutes, covered with a dome of foil, shiny side in.

Drain and use immediately.

Vermicelli

Cooking: Place in a large dish. Cover with plenty of boiling water and add a pinch of salt. Stir well.

Check frequently, stir once or twice and remove when the pasta still has some 'bite'.

Quantity	Time on Full Power			
	600–650w	700–750w	800–850w	900–1000w
225 g/8 oz	5 mins	4½–5 mins	4–4½ mins	4 mins

Standing time: 5 minutes, covered with a dome of foil, shiny side in.

Drain and use immediately.

Long-grain rice

Cooking: Wash the rice thoroughly. Drain and place in a large dish. Add 600 ml/1 pt/2½ cups boiling water (adjust the quantity of water when cooking less rice) and a good pinch of salt. Stir well.

Stir once or twice during cooking and test the grains before the end of the given cooking time. Remove when they give but still have a little' bite'.

Quantity	Time on Full Power			
	600–650w	700–750w	800–850w	900–1000w
225 g/8 oz/ 1 cup	14 mins	12 mins	10 mins	9–10 mins

Standing time: 3 minutes, covered with a dome of foil, shiny side in. The liquid should now all be absorbed.

Fluff up with a fork and serve.

Brown rice

Cooking: Wash the rice, drain and place in a large dish. Add 400 ml/ 14 fl oz/3¾ cups boiling water (adjust the quantity of water for less rice) and a good pinch of salt. Stir well.

Cook on Full Power for 3 minutes, then turn the oven to Medium and cook according to the times given below.

Stir once or twice during cooking.

Quantity	Time on Medium			
	600–650w	700–750w	800–850w	900–1000w
175 g/6 oz/ ¾ cup	40 mins	35 mins	30 mins	25–30 mins

Standing time: 3 minutes, covered with a dome of foil, shiny side in. All the liquid should now be absorbed.

Fluff up with a fork and serve.

Creamy rice pudding

Serves 4

Cooking: For best results, soak the rice in the milk overnight. Put the rice in a large dish. Add a 410 g/14 oz/large can of unsweetened, condensed milk and one canful of water. Stir in 30 ml/2 tbsp sugar.

Microwave on Full Power for 5 minutes, stirring once until boiling. Reduce to Medium, then cook according to the times given below.

Stir several times during cooking and once more before standing.

Quantity	Time on Full Power			
	600–650w	700–750w	800–850w	900–1000w
50 g/1 oz/ ¼ cup	40 mins	35 mins	30 mins	25–30 mins

Standing time: 5 minutes, covered with a dome of foil, shiny side in.

Dust with a little grated nutmeg if liked, before serving.

Flavoured rice dishes

Adjust the quantities of flavourings if you are cooking less rice.

Savoury rice: Cook as either long-grain or brown rice (see page 122), but crumble a chicken, beef or vegetable stock cube into the boiling water.

Fragrant yellow rice: Prepare long-grain rice as on page 122, but add 5 ml/1 tsp turmeric, 1 small bay leaf, a 2.5 cm/1 in piece of cinnamon stick and 4 split cardamom pods with the water. Remove before serving, if preferred.

Italian tomato rice: Prepare long–grain rice as on page 122, but add half water and a 400 g/14 oz/large can of chopped tomatoes instead of all water and stir in 15 ml/1 tbsp tomato purée (paste). After standing, stir in 15 ml/1 tbsp chopped fresh basil before serving.

Vegetable rice: Prepare as for Savoury rice (above), but add 100 g/4 oz/1 cup diced, frozen, mixed vegetables with the boiling water and cook for an extra 1–2 minutes.

Vegetables and Pulses

Vegetables and pulses cook extremely well in the microwave. In the next few pages, you will discover how to prepare and cook most kinds of fresh vegetable. All the nutrients and colour are saved, as very little liquid is needed. It is important to follow the guidelines below and, remember, as with all microwaved foods, they will continue to cook during their standing time, when they should be left covered and undisturbed.

As an added convenience, you can cook your vegetables in advance in microwave-safe serving dishes, then quickly reheat in the microwave before serving without loss of nutrients, colour or flavour.

Microwave tips for vegetables

Peeling baby (pearl) onions or shallots

This will save you lots of time when you are cooking and particularly if you are preparing large quantities for pickling. Place 100 g/4 oz in a bowl. Microwave on Full Power for 1 minute. Leave to stand for 30 seconds, then cut off the root ends and squeeze from the other ends. The skins will slip off.

Peeling garlic cloves

Put whole cloves round the edge of a plate with a small glass of water in the centre. Microwave on Full Power for about 15 seconds per clove until just warm. Snip at one end, then squeeze and they will pop out of their skins.

Cooking frozen vegetables

It is not generally necessary to defrost frozen vegetables before cooking. For best results, follow these general rules.

- Cook on Full Power instead of the normal defrosting power of Medium-Low.

- Allow an extra 1–2 minutes' cooking time compared with fresh vegetables (see the individual vegetables in this chapter).

- Home-frozen vegetables will take a little longer to cook than commercially prepared ones.

- No added water is necessary.

- Always use a covered dish.

- If you need to cook more than 225 g/8 oz frozen vegetables, do it in two batches.

- If the vegetables are in a block, break up gently as soon as possible, and stir once or twice to distribute the heat more evenly.

- If the vegetables were commercially frozen in a bag, there is no need to empty them into a container if cooking the whole lot. Snip the corner off the bag and place it in the oven. Gently flex or shake the bag once or twice during cooking to distribute the heat more evenly. Remove with oven gloves as the bag will soften and get very hot. Pour off any liquid before serving.

Cooking fresh vegetables

- Keep water to a minimum. If you like your vegetables soft, however, add a little extra water and cook for a few seconds longer.

- Vegetables with a high water content, such as spinach, mushrooms and courgettes (zucchini), don't need any extra water. The water clinging to them after washing is sufficient. At most, add 30 ml/2 tbsp.

- Always pierce the skin of whole vegetables, such as jacket potatoes, to prevent bursting.

- Cut vegetables into even-sized pieces for even cooking.

- Arrange with the most delicate parts towards the centre of the dish, e.g. the heads of broccoli or asparagus.

- Always cook in a covered dish. A casserole dish (Dutch oven) with a lid is ideal. This does not apply to jacket potatoes, which should be wrapped individually in kitchen paper (paper towels).

- Stir gently or rearrange once during cooking for more even results.

- Don't try to cook enormous quantities all at once. A shallow, even layer of vegetables will cook quickly and perfectly. Too much and you'll never get them cooked evenly.

- If you wish to add salt, do so at the end of cooking before leaving the vegetables to stand. Salting before cooking will toughen them.

Cooking more than one vegetable at a time

You usually want more than one vegetable with a meal. If you have a divided microwave dish, this is ideal. But you can arrange up to three small dishes in the cooker at one time. Start by cooking the vegetable that takes the longest, then add the others a little later. For instance, if you were cooking new potatoes, carrots and courgettes, put the potatoes in first and start to cook them, add the carrots after a minute or two and then the courgettes. To compensate for the extra quantity of food in the microwave (which will affect the cooking time), add on a minute or two extra at the end.

Stir-frying vegetables

Stir-frying in the microwave takes about the same amount of time as cooking conventionally, but less stirring is needed and cooking smells and any splattering are kept to a minimum. There is also no risk of burning the food. There is no need to heat the oil first. Simply toss the first foods to be cooked (see below) in a little oil in a large, shallow dish. Microwave on Full Power for 2 minutes, then add the other vegetables, stirring every 1 minute until cooked to your liking. Season with soy sauce, spices, sherry, etc. at the end. For best results, follow these general rules.

- Cut food into even-sized pieces.

- A vegetable stir-fry for four people will take about 4–6 minutes.

- Start with the vegetables that take longest to cook, e.g. onions, carrots, celery, then add the remainder, e.g. (bell) peppers, courgettes (zucchini), cucumber, mushrooms, beansprouts and so on.

- If adding Chinese noodles, cook according to the packet instructions, drain and add at the end of the cooking time. Microwave on Full Power for 1 further minute to heat through. Toss before serving.

- If using meat, cook for 2–3 minutes on Full Power, stirring once, until almost cooked, before adding the vegetables.

Cooking pulses (dried beans, peas and lentils)

All pulses, except red lentils, should be soaked for several hours or overnight in cold water before microwaving. The only advantage of cooking in the microwave rather than conventionally is that they won't boil dry and burn. Drain after soaking, place in a very large bowl, cover with enough boiling water to come 2.5 cm/1 in above the beans. Microwave for 30 minutes, then stir. Always use Full Power, as the water must boil rapidly during cooking to destroy any toxins in the beans. Test for tenderness, then continue to cook in 5-minute bursts until tender but still holding their shape. Stir after each burst. Season with salt, if liked, and leave to stand for 5 minutes, then drain and use as required. Never add salt before cooking as it toughens the skins.

Red lentils do not need to be soaked before cooking. Cover with boiling water and cook for 20 minutes. Test and cook for a little longer, if necessary, until tender. Season with salt, if liked, when cooked. Leave to stand for 5 minutes, then drain and use as required.

Cooking times for fresh vegetables

Artichokes, globe

Cooking: Twist off stalks and trim the points of the leaves, if liked.
Arrange in a circle in a casserole dish (Dutch oven).
Add 60 ml/4 tbsp water. Cover.

Rearrange once or twice during cooking.

Quantity	Time on Medium–High			
	600–650w	700–750w	800–850w	900–1000w
1	6 mins	5½ mins	4½–5 mins	4¼ mins
2	9 mins	8 mins	7 mins	6½–7 mins
3	13 mins	11½ mins	10 mins	9½–10 mins
4	17 mins	14 mins	13 mins	12–13 mins

Standing time: 4 minutes, covered. A leaf should then pull away easily.
Season with salt if liked.

Artichokes, Jerusalem

Cooking: Scrub or peel. Cut into chunks. Place in a casserole dish (Dutch
oven). Add 60 ml/4 tbsp water and a squeeze of lemon juice and cover.

Stir once or twice during cooking.

Quantity	Time on Full Power			
	600–650w	700–750w	800–850w	900–1000w
225 g/ 8 oz	4–6 mins	3½–5 mins	3–4 mins	2½–3 mins
450 g/1 lb	6–8 mins	5–7 mins	4–5½ mins	3½–4 mins

Standing time: 3 minutes, covered.
Season with salt, if liked.

Asparagus

Cooking: Trim the stalks. Scrape the stems if thick. Arrange in an even
layer in a casserole dish (Dutch oven). Add 60 ml/4 tbsp water and cover.

Gently rearrange once during cooking.

Quantity	Time on Full Power			
	600–650w	700–750w	800–850w	900–1000w
225 g/8 oz	4 mins	3½ mins	3 mins	2½–3 mins
450 g/1 lb	8 mins	7 mins	5½–6 mins	5½ mins

Standing time: 3 minutes, covered.
Season with salt, if liked.

Aubergines (eggplants)

Cooking: Trim off stalks and slice or dice. Place in a colander and sprinkle with salt. Leave to stand for 15 minutes, then rinse and drain well. Place in an even layer in a casserole dish (Dutch oven). Add 90 ml/6 tbsp water. Cover.

Stir once or twice during cooking.

Quantity	Time on Full Power			
	600–650w	700–750w	800–850w	900–1000w
225 g/8 oz	3–4 mins	2½–3½ mins	2–3 mins	2 mins
450 g/1 lb	6–8 mins	5–7 mins	4–6 mins	3½–5 mins

Standing time: 2 minutes, covered.

Broad (fava) beans

Cooking: Shell. Place in an even layer in a casserole dish (Dutch oven). Add 60 ml/4 tbsp water. Cover.

Stir once or twice during cooking.

Quantity	Time on Full Power			
	600–650w	700–750w	800–850w	900–1000w
225 g/8 oz, shelled weight	6 mins	5 mins	4 mins	3½ mins
450 g/1 lb, shelled weight	10 mins	9 mins	7½ mins	7 mins

Standing time: 4 minutes, covered.
Season with salt, if liked.

Flat beans

Cooking: Top and tail. Cut into chunky pieces or slice diagonally.
Place in an even layer in a casserole dish (Dutch oven).
Add 60–90 ml/4–6 tbsp water, depending on the quantity. Cover.

Stir once or twice during cooking.

Quantity	Time on Full Power			
	600–650w	700–750w	800–850w	900–1000w
225 g/8 oz	7–8 mins	6–7 mins	5–6 mins	4½–5½ mins
450 g/1 lb	14–16 mins	12–13 mins	10–11 mins	9½–10½ mins

Standing time: 4 minutes, covered.
Season with salt, if liked.

French (green) beans

Cooking: Top and tail, then leave whole or cut into short lengths. Place in
an even layer in a casserole dish (Dutch oven).
Add 60–90 ml/4–6 tbsp water, depending on the quantity. Cover.

Stir once or twice during cooking.

Quantity	Time on Full Power			
	600–650w	700–750w	800–850w	900–1000w
225 g/8 oz	7–8 mins	6–7 mins	5–6 mins	4½–5½ mins
450 g/1 lb	14–16 mins	12–13 mins	10–11 mins	9½–10½ mins

Standing time: 4 minutes, covered.
Season with salt, if liked.

Runner beans

Cooking: String the beans and cut into diagonal slices. Place in an even
layer in a casserole dish (Dutch oven). Add 60–90 ml/4–6 tbsp water,
depending on the quantity. Cover.

Stir once or twice during cooking.

Quantity	Time on Full Power			
	600–650w	700–750w	800–850w	900–1000w
225 g/8 oz	7–8 mins	6–7 mins	5–6 mins	4½–5½ mins
450 g/1 lb	14–16 mins	12–13 mins	10–11 mins	9½–10½ mins

Standing time: 4 minutes, covered.
Season with salt, if liked.

Beetroot (red beets)

Cooking: Wash but do not peel. Place in a casserole dish (Dutch oven). Pour in enough boiling water to cover the vegetables. Cover.

Rearrange twice during cooking.

Quantity	Time on Medium-High			
	600 650w	700–750w	800–850w	900–1000w
12 baby or 4 medium	22–24 mins	19–21 mins	16–18 mins	15–17 mins

Standing time: 8 minutes, covered.

Peel before use.

Broccoli

Cooking: Separate into even-sized florets. Place in a casserole dish (Dutch oven), with the heads towards the centre of the dish. Add 45 ml/ 3 tbsp water. Cover.

Rearrange once during cooking.

Quantity	Time on Full Power			
	600–650w	700–750w	800–850w	900–1000w
225 g/8 oz	8–9 mins	7½–8½ mins	6–7 mins	5½–6½ mins

Standing time: 3 minutes, covered.
Season with salt, if liked.

Brussels sprouts

Cooking: Choose even-sized sprouts. Peel off damaged outer leaves. Make a cross-cut into the stalks. Place in an even layer in a casserole dish (Dutch oven). Add 45 ml/3 tbsp water. Cover.

Stir gently once or twice during cooking.

Quantity	Time on Full Power			
	600–650w	700–750w	800–850w	900–1000w
225 g/8 oz	4–6 mins	3½–5 mins	3–4 mins	2½–3½ mins
450 g/1 lb	8–10 mins	7–8½ mins	5½–7 mins	5–6 mins

Standing time: 3 minutes, covered.
Season with salt, if liked.

Cabbage

Cooking: Remove any damaged outer leaves and thick stump. Shred the cabbage. Place in an even layer in a casserole dish (Dutch oven). Add 45 ml/3 tbsp water. Cover.

Stir gently once or twice during cooking.

Quantity	Time on Full Power			
	600–650w	700–750w	800–850w	900–1000w
1 medium	8–9 mins	7–8 mins	6–7 mins	5½–6½ mins

Standing time: 3 minutes, covered.
Season with salt, if liked.

Carrots

Cooking: Scrub or peel. Cut into slices or matchsticks. Place in an even layer in a casserole dish (Dutch oven). Add 45–90 ml/3–6 tbsp water, depending on the quantity. Cover.

Stir gently once or twice during cooking.

Quantity	Time on Full Power			
	600–650w	700–750w	800–850w	900–1000w
225 g/8 oz	7–9 mins	6–8 mins	5–7 mins	4½–6 mins
450 g/1 lb	14–16 mins	12–14 mins	10–12 mins	9–11 mins

Standing time: 3 minutes, covered.
Season with salt, if liked.

Cauliflower

Cooking: Trim and separate into even-sized florets. Arrange with the heads towards the centre of a casserole dish (Dutch oven). Add 90 ml/6 tbsp water. Cover.

Rearrange once or twice during cooking.

Quantity	Time on Full Power			
	600–650w	700–750w	800–850w	900–1000w
1 medium	10–12 mins	9–11 mins	8–10 mins	7–9 mins

Standing time: 3 minutes, covered.
Season with salt, if liked.

Celeriac (celery root)

Cooking: Peel and cut into matchsticks. Place in an even layer in a casserole dish (Dutch oven). Add 60 ml/4 tbsp water and 5 ml/1 tsp lemon juice. Cover.

Stir gently once or twice during cooking.

Quantity	Time on Full Power			
	600–650w	700–750w	800–850w	900–1000w
1 medium	8–9 mins	7–8 mins	6–7 mins	5½–6½ mins

Standing time: 3 minutes, covered.
Season with salt, if liked.

Celery

Cooking: Scrub, then slice or chop. Place in an even layer in a casserole dish (Dutch oven). Add 45 ml/3 tbsp water. Cover.

Stir gently once or twice during cooking.

Quantity	Time on Full Power			
	600–650w	700–750w	800–850w	900–1000w
1 head	9–10 mins	8–9 mins	7–8 mins	6½–7½ mins

Standing time: 2 minutes, covered.
Season with salt, if liked.

Corn on the cob

Cooking: Cook no more than two at a time.
Remove husks and silks. Trim stalks. Place head to stalk in a casserole dish (Dutch oven). Add 45 ml/3 tbsp water and cover. Alternatively, wrap individually in buttered greaseproof (waxed) paper.

Turn once during cooking.

Quantity	Time on Full Power			
	600–650w	700–750w	800–850w	900–1000w
2	7–9 mins	6–8 mins	5–7 mins	4–5 mins

Standing time: 2 minutes, covered.

Courgettes (zucchini)

Cooking: Trim, then slice or cut into matchsticks.
Place in an even layer in a casserole dish (Dutch oven). Add 30 ml/2 tbsp water or a good knob of butter with a crushed garlic clove. Cover.

Stir once or twice during cooking.

Quantity	Time on Full Power			
	600–650w	700–750w	800–850w	900–1000w
2 medium	6 mins	5 mins	4 mins	3½–4 mins

Standing time: 3 minutes, covered.
Season with salt, if liked.

Fennel

Cooking: Trim the feathery fronds and reserve for garnish, if liked. Slice or cut into small wedges. Place in an even layer in a casserole dish (Dutch oven). Add 60 ml/4 tbsp water. Cover.

Stir once or twice during cooking.

Quantity	Time on Full Power			
	600–650w	700–750w	800–850w	900–1000w
1 bulb	6 mins	5 mins	4 mins	3½–4 mins

Standing time: 3 minutes, covered.
Season with salt, if liked.

Kale

Cooking: Discard the thick stalks and shred the leaves. Place in an even layer in a casserole dish (Dutch oven).
Add 45–90 ml/3–6 tbsp water, depending on the quantity. Cover.

Stir once or twice during cooking.

Quantity	Time on Full Power			
	600–650w	700–750w	800–850w	900–1000w
225 g/8 oz	4–6 mins	3½–5 mins	3–4 mins	2½–3 mins
450 g/1 lb	8–10 mins	7–9 mins	6–8 mins	5–7 mins

Standing time: 3 minutes, covered.
Season with salt, if liked.

Kohl rabi

Cooking: Peel and cut into chunks. Place in an even layer in a casserole dish (Dutch oven). Add 45 ml/3 tbsp water. Cover.

Stir once or twice during cooking.

Quantity	Time on Full Power			
	600–650w	700–750w	800–850w	900–1000w
2 medium	16 mins	14 mins	12 mins	11 mins

Standing time: 3 minutes, covered.
Season with salt, if liked.

Leeks

Cooking: Trim, wash thoroughly and slice. If small and thin, leave whole.
Place in an even layer in a casserole dish (Dutch oven).
Add 45 ml/3 tbsp water. Cover.

Quantity	Time on Full Power			
	600–650w	700–750w	800–850w	900–1000w
2 medium or 4 small	6–7 mins	5–6 mins	4–5 mins	3½–4 mins

Standing time: 3 minutes, covered.
Season with salt, if liked.

Mangetout (snow peas)

Cooking: Top and tail but leave whole. Place in an even layer in a
casserole dish (Dutch oven). Add 60 ml/4 tbsp water. Cover.

Stir once or twice during cooking.

Quantity	Time on Full Power			
	600–650w	700–750w	800–850w	900–1000w
225 g/8 oz	4 mins	3½ mins	3 mins	2½–3 mins

Standing time: 2 minutes, covered.
Season with salt, if liked.

Marrow (squash)

Cooking: Cut into thick slices, remove the seeds, peel and halve or
quarter the slices. Cut into dice, if liked. Place in an even layer in a
casserole dish (Dutch oven). Add 60 ml/4 tbsp water. Cover.

Quantity	Time on Full Power			
	600–650w	700–750w	800–850w	900–1000w
1 small	7–8 mins	6–7 mins	5–6 mins	4½–5 mins

Standing time: 3 minutes, covered.
Season with salt, if liked.

Mushrooms, button and cup varieties

Cooking: Wipe, trim and slice if large, or leave whole. Place in an even layer in a casserole dish (Dutch oven). Add a knob of butter, if liked. Cover.

Stir once during cooking.

Quantity	Time on Full Power			
	600–650w	700–750w	800–850w	900–1000w
225 g/8 oz	3–4 mins	2½–3½ mins	2–3 mins	2 mins

Standing time: 3 minutes, covered.
Season with salt, if liked.

Mushrooms, large flat varieties

Cooking: Wipe, peel if necessary and trim the stalks. Place in a single layer in a casserole dish (Dutch oven). Add 30 ml/2 tbsp water or wine and dot each with a knob of butter. Add a crushed garlic clove, if liked. Cover.

Quantity	Time on Full Power			
	600–650w	700–750w	800–850w	900–1000w
6	3–4 mins	2½–3½ mins	2–3 mins	2 mins

Standing time: 3 minutes, covered.
Season with salt, if liked.

Okra (ladies' fingers)

Cooking: Wash, trim but leave whole. Place in an even layer in a casserole dish (Dutch oven). Cover.

Shake the dish once or twice during cooking.

Quantity	Time on Full Power			
	600–650w	700–750w	800–850w	900–1000w
225 g/8 oz	5 mins	4 mins	3½ mins	3–3½ mins

Standing time: 3 minutes, covered.
Season with salt, if liked.

Onions, baby (pearl)

Cooking: Trim the root ends, then peel but leave whole. Place in an even layer in a casserole dish (Dutch oven). Cover.

Stir gently once or twice during cooking.

Quantity	Time on Full Power			
	600–650w	700–750w	800–850w	900–1000w
225 g/8 oz	7–9 mins	6–8 mins	5½–6½ mins	5–6 mins

Standing time: 3 minutes, covered.

Onions, chopped or sliced

Cooking: Trim the root ends, then peel, halve and slice or chop. Place in a bowl. Add either 15 ml/1 tbsp water or a good knob of butter. There is no need to cover.

Stir once or twice during cooking.

Quantity	Time on Full Power			
	600–650w	700–750w	800–850w	900–1000w
1 medium	3½–4½ mins	3–4 mins	2½–3 mins	2–2½ mins
1 large	7 mins	6 mins	5 mins	4½ mins

Standing time: 2 minutes.

Parsnips

Cooking: Peel and slice or dice. Place in an even layer in a casserole dish (Dutch oven). Add 60 ml/4 tbsp water. Cover.

Stir once or twice during cooking.

Quantity	Time on Full Power			
	600–650w	700–750w	800–850w	900–1000w
225 g/8 oz	3–4 mins	2½–3½ mins	2–2½ mins	2 mins
450 g/1 lb	6–8 mins	5–7 mins	4–5 mins	3½–4 mins

Standing time: 3 minutes, covered.
Season with salt, if liked.

Peas

Cooking: Shell. Place in an even layer in a casserole dish (Dutch oven). Add 45 ml/3 tbsp water and a sprig of mint (optional). Cover.

Stir once or twice during cooking.

Quantity	Time on Full Power			
	600–650w	700–750w	800–850w	900–1000w
225 g/8 oz, shelled weight	6 mins	5 mins	4 mins	3½ mins

Standing time: 2 minutes, covered.
Season with salt, if liked.

(Bell) peppers

Cooking: Halve, remove the stalk end and seeds and cut into thin strips Place in an even layer in a casserole dish (Dutch oven). Add 15–30 ml/1–2 tbsp oil. Do not cover.

Stir two or three times during cooking.

Quantity	Time on Full Power			
	600–650w	700–750w	800–850w	900–1000w
2	3–4 mins	2½–3½ mins	2–3 mins	1½–2½ mins

Standing time: 2 minutes, covered.

Potatoes, boiled

Cooking: Scrub or peel. Cut into chunks or leave whole if small. Place in an even layer in a casserole dish (Dutch oven). Add 45 ml/3 tbsp water and a sprig of mint, if liked. Cover.

Stir gently once or twice during cooking.

Quantity	Time on Full Power			
	600–650w	700–750w	800–850w	900–1000w
450 g/1 lb	12 mins	10 mins	8 mins	7–8 mins

Standing time: 3 minutes, covered.
Season with salt, if liked.

Potatoes, in their jackets

Cooking: Scrub and prick the skins. Wrap individually in kitchen paper (paper towels). Place in a ring on a microwave rack or on the turntable.

Turn once during cooking.

Quantity	Time on Full Power			
	600–650w	700–750w	800–850w	900–1000w
1 large	5 mins	4½ mins	4 mins	3½–4 mins
2 large	9–10 mins	8–9 mins	7½–8 mins	7–7½ mins
3 large	13½–15 mins	12–13½ mins	11–12 mins	10–11 mins
4 large	17½–20 mins	16–18 mins	14½–16 mins	14–15 mins

Standing time: 4–5 minutes, wrapped in foil, shiny side in, or a clean cloth. They will stay hot for up to an hour if covered in foil **and** a cloth.

Potatoes, sweet

Cooking: Peel and cut into chunks. Place in a casserole dish (Dutch oven). Add 60 ml/4 tbsp water. Cover.

Stir once or twice during cooking.

Quantity	Time on Full Power			
	600–650w	700–750w	800–850w	900–1000w
450 g/1 lb	10 mins	9 mins	8 mins	7½–8 mins

Standing time: 3 minutes, covered.
Season with salt, if liked. Mash with a knob of butter and some pepper.

Salsify

Cooking: Wash and scrape. Cut into chunks. Place in an even layer in a casserole dish (Dutch oven). Add 60 ml/4 tbsp water. Cover.

Quantity	Time on Full Power			
	600–650w	700–750w	800–850w	900–1000w
1 medium	12 mins	11 mins	10 mins	9½ mins

Standing time: 3 minutes, covered.
Season with salt, if liked.

Spinach

Cooking: Wash thoroughly. Discard any tough stalks. Place in a casserole dish (Dutch oven). Do not add any water. Cover.

Stir once or twice during cooking.

Quantity	Time on Full Power			
	600–650w	700–750w	800–850w	900–1000w
225 g/8 oz	5 mins	4–4½ mins	3–4 mins	2–3 mins

Standing time: 3 minutes, covered.
Season with salt, if liked.

Spring (collard) greens

Cooking: Wash well and discard any thick stalks. Shred the leaves.
Place in an even layer in a casserole dish (Dutch oven).
Add 45 ml/3 tbsp water. Cover.

Quantity	Time on Full Power			
	600–650w	700–750w	800–850w	900–1000w
225 g/8 oz	4–6 mins	3½–5 mins	3–4 mins	2½–3 mins
450 g/1 lb	10 mins	8–9 mins	6–7 mins	6 mins

Standing time: 3 minutes, covered.
Season with salt, if liked.

Swede (rutabaga)

Cooking: Peel and cut into chunks. Place in an even layer in a casserole dish (Dutch oven). Add 60 ml/4 tbsp water. Cover.

Stir once or twice during cooking.

Quantity	Time on Full Power			
	600–650w	700–750w	800–850w	900–1000w
1 medium	8–10 mins	6–7 mins	5–6 mins	5 mins

Standing time: 3 minutes, covered.
Season with salt, if liked. Mash and add a knob
of butter and some pepper.

Swiss chard

Cooking: Cut off the white stalks, trim and cut into neat lengths. Shred the leaves. Place the stalks and leaves in an even layer in a casserole dish (Dutch oven). Add 60 ml/4 tbsp water. Cover.

Quantity	Time on Full Power			
	600–650w	700–750w	800–850w	900–1000w
450 g/1 lb	8–10 mins	6–8 mins	5–6 mins	5 mins

Standing time: 3 minutes, covered.
Season with salt, if liked.

Turnips

Cooking: Peel and cut into chunks. Leave baby ones whole. Place in a layer in a casserole dish (Dutch oven). Add 60 ml/4 tbsp water. Cover.

Stir once or twice during cooking.

Quantity	Time on Full Power			
	600–650w	700–750w	800–850w	900–1000w
225 g/8 oz	5 mins	4 mins	3 mins	2½–3 mins
450 g/1 lb	8 mins	7 mins	6 mins	5½ mins

Standing time: 3 minutes, covered.
Season with salt, if liked.

Yams

Cooking: Peel and dice. Place in an even layer in a casserole dish (Dutch oven). Add 60 ml/4 tbsp water. Cover.

Stir once or twice during cooking.

Quantity	Time on Full Power			
	600–650w	700–750w	800–850w	900–1000w
450 g/1 lb	10 mins	9 mins	8 mins	7½–8 mins

Standing time: 3 minutes, covered.
Season with salt, if liked. Mash with a knob of butter and some pepper, if liked.

Fruit and Nuts

Fruit of all kinds cook beautifully in the microwave. You can stew, poach, bake and even bottle them. You can also frost them with sugar and turn them into glacé (candied) fruits. But your microwave is also an absolute boon when it comes to messy little tasks such as skinning fruit, and can even be used for making them juicier and plumping them up if they're dried. There are hints for nuts, too – for toasting, blanching, shelling and roasting. Note that you should use at least 100 g/4 oz/1 cup of nuts in each case – smaller quantities burn too easily.

Note: Don't attempt to dry fruit in the microwave. The high sugar content would make them burn before they are dried.

Microwave tips for fruit and nuts

Juicy citrus fruits
To get the maximum amount of juice from citrus fruit, place in the microwave and cook on Medium-High for 30 seconds to 1 minute per fruit depending on size until just warm. They will then yield more juice than when straight from the fridge or fruit bowl.

To plump up dried fruit
Sultanas (golden raisins), raisins, currants and mixed dried fruit (fruit cake mix) for use in cakes and puddings are even more delicious when plumped up before use. Place in a bowl and add any alcohol or juice from the recipe. Cover with a plate. Microwave on Full Power until the fruit feels hot and has absorbed the liquid, checking and stirring every minute. Stir again and leave to stand until cold.

To skin soft fruits, such as peaches, apricots and tomatoes
Microwave each piece of fruit for 10–15 seconds on Full Power. Leave to stand for 30 seconds, then peel off the skin.

To ripen hard fruit

This is particularly suitable for avocados. Put the unpeeled fruit in the microwave, one at a time, and microwave on Full Power for 1 minute, turning over after 30 seconds. Leave to stand until completely cold, then use as required.

To shell nuts

Place up to 175 g/6 oz nuts in their shells in a bowl. Add 60 ml/ 4 tbsp water and cover with a plate. Microwave on Full Power for 2–3 minutes. Leave to stand for 1 minute, then drain. The shells can be removed easily.

To roast whole nuts

Place 100 g/4 oz/1 cup raw, shelled nuts in a shallow dish. Stir in 15 ml/1 tbsp sunflower or peanut (groundnut) oil and spread out evenly. Microwave on Full Power for 3–5 minutes, stirring after every minute until evenly brown. Turn on to kitchen paper (paper towels) and leave to cool. Sprinkle with salt, if liked. Store in an airtight container.

To dry-roast whole nuts

Spread 100 g/4 oz/1 cup raw, shelled nuts out on a piece of kitchen paper (paper towels) in a shallow dish. Do not add any oil. Microwave on Full Power for 3–5 minutes, tossing after every minute, until browned. Leave until cold, then store in an airtight container.

Spiced roasted nuts: Dry-roast the nuts as above, then sprinkle with sea salt and chilli powder to taste. Leave to cool, then store in an airtight container.

Savoury salty nuts: Dry-roast them but sprinkle with 30 ml/ 2 tbsp soy sauce halfway through cooking, and toss well to coat.

To toast nuts

Toasted nuts are good for adding colour and texture to microwaved foods. Spread 100 g/4 oz/1 cup flaked (slivered) or chopped raw nuts on a piece of kitchen paper (paper towels) in a shallow dish. Microwave on Full Power, stirring every minute until golden, then remove from the microwave immediately. Take care, as being thin and small, they burn easily so do not overcook. If necessary, stand a small cup of water in the oven with the nuts to absorb some of the energy.

To shell nuts

Hard-shelled nuts, such as brazils, almonds and walnuts, can be softened slightly by placing in a shallow dish and adding just enough water to cover. Microwave on Full Power until the water boils. Remove from the oven immediately. Leave to stand for 1 minute, then drain. Spread out on kitchen paper (paper towels) to dry, then shell in the usual way.

To blanch almonds

Place 100 g/4 oz/1 cup almonds with their skins on in a bowl and add 150 ml/¼ pt/⅔ cup water. Microwave on Full Power for 1½ to 2½ minutes. Drain and when cool enough to handle, slip off the skins between your finger and thumb.

To blanch hazelnuts (filberts)

Spread the hazelnuts in their skins in a single layer in a shallow dish. Microwave on Full Power for 1½ to 2½ minutes. Tip into a clean tea towel (dishcloth) and rub off the skins.

Defrosting frozen fruits

Frozen fruits should be partially defrosted in the microwave, then left to finish defrosting at room temperature. Otherwise, because of their high sugar content, they will cook before properly defrosted. For best results, follow these general rules.

• Free-flow, commercially frozen fruit is best defrosted at room temperature unless you are heating straight from frozen.

• For fruit home-frozen in dry sugar, allow 2 minutes per 450 g/1 lb on Full Power, then leave to defrost at room temperature.

• For fruit frozen in syrup, allow 4 minutes per 450 g/1 lb on Full Power, then leave to defrost at room temperature.

• For fruit frozen as purée, allow 2 minutes per 450 g/1 lb, then leave to defrost at room temperature.

Cooking fruit

With so many fruits and berries of all kinds now available all the year round, it is quick and simple to prepare a delicious dessert with the help of your microwave.

Both fresh and dried fruits microwave well and can be used as a base for steamed puddings and crumbles, ice creams, sauces and purées. As with vegetables, fruits retain a high percentage of their flavour and colour when cooked in a microwave oven. Here are the basic guidelines.

- Hard fruits, such as apples and pears, should be peeled and cored in the usual way. Cut the fruit into even-sized pieces and sprinkle with sugar to taste. There is no need to add liquid – the fruit will cook in its own juice.

- Plums, cherries, greengages and damsons should be halved and stoned (pitted). Cherries can be left whole if you have a cherry stoner.

- Peaches, nectarines and apricots don't need skinning before you microwave them: the skins will peel away afterwards. Cut the fruit into halves, remove the stones (pits) and sprinkle with sugar to taste.

- Berry fruits, such as red and black currants and gooseberries, cook particularly well in the microwave. Shred currants off their stalks using the prongs of a fork and top and tail gooseberries. Wash the fruit in the usual way.

- Add only a little sugar before cooking berry fruits. You can always add more after cooking, but you can't take it out if you've over-sweetened them.

- Vanilla sugar (sugar flavoured by being stored in a jar with a vanilla pod) adds delicious flavour.

To stew fruit

Peel, core slice and remove stones (pits) as necessary. Place in an even layer in a casserole dish (Dutch oven). Sprinkle with sugar. Water is not necessary, but you can add up to 30 ml/2 tbsp water for extra juice. As a rough guide, soft fruits take 2–5 minutes, hard fruits 6–10 minutes (see individual entries). Test and stir after 2 minutes, then after each further minute until cooked to your liking. Taste and add more sugar as necessary.

To poach fruit

Skin the fruit, if liked, or prick the skins to prevent bursting. Leave whole or cut into halves and remove any stones (pits). For each 450 g/1 lb fruit, make 1 quantity of sugar syrup as follows.

Stir 100 g/4 oz/½ cup granulated sugar into 300 ml/½ pt/ 1¼ cups water in a casserole dish (Dutch oven). Add a thick slice of lemon. Microwave on Full Power for 3–5 minutes until boiling and the sugar has dissolved, stirring after every minute. Alternatively, use 300 ml/½ pt/¼ cups pure apple juice.

Add the fruit in an even layer. Cover. Microwave on Full Power for the time indicated in individual entries, turning the fruit over in the syrup once during cooking. Leave to stand for 2 minutes. Do not overcook or the fruit will disintegrate.

Frosted fruits

You can frost small bunches of grapes and red, black or white currants for use as decoration on desserts.

Lightly beat an egg white. Dip small bunches of fruit in the egg white, draining off any excess. Dip gently in caster (superfine) sugar, dusting the fruit all over until completely coated. Place in a circle on a sheet of non-stick baking parchment on a microwave rack or a plate. Microwave on Medium-Low until the frosting is dry and hard. Turn the fruit over after 1½ minutes. 6–8 small bunches will take 3–4 minutes.

Glacé (candied) fruits

Choose fresh fruit, such as strawberries, orange, clementine or satsuma segments, grapes, cherries, lychees, kumquats, sliced peaches or nectarines or pieces of pineapple, dried on kitchen paper (paper towels). You can also use canned fruits but they must be drained and dried thoroughly on kitchen paper.

Put 100 g/4 oz/½ cup granulated sugar and 75 ml/5 tbsp boiling water in a large measuring jug. Microwave on Full Power for 1 minute, then stir. Whisk in 5 ml/1 tsp powdered glucose and microwave for 1 further minute. Stir until the sugar dissolves completely. Microwave on Full Power for a further 5–7 minutes, checking frequently, until the syrup is just beginning to turn golden – no more. Immediately stand the base of the jug in cold water to cool it quickly. Using a cocktail stick (toothpick), pierce a piece of fruit, dip it in the syrup, allowing the excess to run off, then place on a piece of non-stick baking parchment to dry. Place in paper sweet cases (candy cups) before serving.

To bottle fruit

Prepare the fruit in your usual way, using the microwave for each step as follows.

Boil the syrup on Full Power for 2–3 minutes.

To sterilise the jars, put 150 ml/¼ pt/⅔ cup water in each one. Cook on Full Power until the water boils, then microwave for a further minute. Using oven-gloved hands, pour out the water and drain upside down on kitchen paper (paper towels).

Fill the jars with the prepared fruit and cook one filled jar at a time on Full Power for 2–3 minutes until the syrup boils. Turn the microwave down to Medium-Low and microwave for a further 3–4 minutes. Remove with oven gloves. Cover, seal and label.

Cooking times for fruit

Apples, cooking (tart)

Cooking: Peel, core and thinly slice. Put in a thin layer in a shallow dish or casserole dish (Dutch oven). Sprinkle with sugar to taste and add a pinch of cinnamon, cloves, mixed (apple-pie) spice or the grated rind of a lemon or orange. Dot with a few flakes of butter, if liked. Cover with clingfilm (plastic wrap), rolled back at one edge, or a lid.

Stir gently once during cooking to rearrange the slices without breaking up.

For purée (apple sauce), you can stir more briskly, then beat well after standing time, pass through a sieve (strainer) or purée in a blender or food processor.

Quantity	Time on Full Power			
	600–650w	700–750w	800–850w	900–1000w
225 g/8 oz	3–4 mins	2½–3½ mins	2–3 mins	1½–2 mins
450 g/1 lb	6–8 mins	5–7 mins	4–5½ mins	3½–4 mins

Standing time: 2 minutes.

Baked whole apples

Cooking: Core the apples but do not peel. Mark around the circumference of each apple with a sharp knife to prevent splitting. Arrange around the edge of a shallow dish. Fill the centres with a little brown sugar mixed with mixed dried fruit (fruit cake mix), or other stuffing of your choice. Do not cover.

Quantity	Time on Full Power			
	600–650w	700–750w	800–850w	900–1000w
2	5 mins	4 mins	3½ mins	3–3½ mins
4	10 mins	7½–8 mins	7 mins	6½–7 mins

Once cooked, pour a little golden (light corn) syrup over or sprinkle with a little more sugar.

Standing time: 5 minutes, covered with foil, shiny side in.

Apricots

Cooking: Wash, halve and remove the stones (pits). Put in a thin layer in a shallow dish or casserole dish (Dutch oven). Sprinkle with sugar, to taste.

Stir gently once or twice during cooking to coat in the juice.

Quantity	Time on Full Power			
	600–650w	700–750w	800–850w	900–1000w
225 g/8 oz	2–3 mins	1½–2½ mins	1–2 mins	1–1½ mins
450 g/1 lb	4–5 mins	3½–4 mins	3–3½ mins	2½–3 mins

Standing time: 2 minutes.

Bananas

Cooking: Peel and halve lengthways. Put in a single layer in a shallow dish or casserole dish (Dutch oven). Sprinkle with 5 ml/1 tsp light brown sugar per banana. Add a little rum, or grated rind and juice of an orange or lemon. Cover with clingfilm (plastic wrap), rolled back at one edge, or a lid.

Quantity	Time on Full Power			
	600–650w	700–750w	800–850w	900–1000w
4	6 mins	5 mins	4 mins	3½–4 mins

Standing time: 2 minutes.

Blackberries

Cooking: Wash and remove any stalks. Put in a thin layer in a shallow dish or casserole dish (Dutch oven). Sprinkle with sugar, to taste. Add the grated rind of an orange, if liked. Cover with clingfilm (plastic wrap), rolled back at one edge, or a lid.

Stir gently once during cooking.

Quantity	Time on Full Power			
	600–650w	700–750w	800–850w	900–1000w
225 g/8 oz	2–2½ mins	1½–2 mins	1–1½ mins	1 min
450 g/1 lb	3–5 mins	2½–4 mins	2–3 mins	2 mins

Standing time: 2 minutes.

Blackcurrants

Cooking: Wash the fruit and strip off the stalks with the prongs of a fork. Put in a thin layer in a shallow dish or casserole dish (Dutch oven). Sprinkle with sugar, to taste. Cover with clingfilm (plastic wrap), rolled back at one edge, or a lid.

Stir or shake gently once or twice during cooking.

Quantity	Time on Full Power			
	600–650w	700–750w	800–850w	900–1000w
225 g/8 oz	2–2½ mins	1½–2 mins	1–1½ mins	1 min
450 g/1 lb	3–5 mins	2½–4 mins	2–3 mins	2 mins

Standing time: 2 minutes.

Blueberries

Cooking: Wash the fruit. Put in a thin layer in a shallow dish or casserole dish (Dutch oven). Sprinkle with sugar, to taste. Cover with clingfilm (plastic wrap), rolled back at one edge, or a lid.

Stir or shake gently once or twice during cooking.

Quantity	Time on Full Power			
	600–650w	700–750w	800–850w	900–1000w
225 g/8 oz	2–2½ mins	1½–2 mins	1–1½ mins	1 min
450 g/1 lb	3–5 mins	2½–4 mins	2–3 mins	2 mins

Standing time: 2 minutes.

Cherries

Cooking: Wash, then halve and stone (pit) the fruit or use a cherry stoner. Put in a thin layer in a shallow dish or casserole dish (Dutch oven). Sprinkle with sugar, to taste. Cover with clingfilm (plastic wrap), rolled back at one edge, or a lid.

Stir or shake gently once or twice during cooking.

Quantity	Time on Full Power			
	600–650w	700–750w	800–850w	900–1000w
225 g/8 oz	2–3 mins	1½–2½ mins	1–2 mins	1–1½ mins
450 g/1 lb	4–5 mins	3½–4 mins	3–3½ mins	2½–3 mins

Standing time: 2 minutes.

Cranberries

Cooking: Wash the fruit. Put in a thin layer in a shallow dish or casserole dish (Dutch oven). Sprinkle with sugar, to taste. Add the grated rind of an orange, if liked. Cover with clingfilm (plastic wrap), rolled back at one edge, or a lid.

Stir or shake gently once or twice during cooking. They will 'pop' when cooked.

Quantity	Time on Full Power			
	600–650w	700–750w	800–850w	900–1000w
225 g/8 oz	2–2½ mins	1½–2 mins	1–1½ mins	1 min

Standing time: 2 minutes.

Damsons

Cooking: Wash, halve and remove the stones (pits).
Put in a thin layer in a shallow dish or casserole dish (Dutch oven).
Sprinkle with sugar, to taste.

Stir gently once or twice during cooking to coat in the juice.

Quantity	Time on Full Power			
	600–650w	700–750w	800–850w	900–1000w
225 g/8 oz	2–3 mins	1½–2½ mins	1–2 mins	1–1½ mins
450 g/1 lb	4–5 mins	3½–4 mins	3–3½ mins	2½–3 mins

Standing time: 2 minutes.

Dried fruit

This method is suitable for larger dried fruit, such as apricots, prunes, peaches, pears and dried fruit salad.

Cooking: Put in a casserole dish (Dutch oven).
Cover with 300 ml/½ pt/1¼ cups orange juice, cold tea or water.
Flavour with a cinnamon stick, a clove or a few drops of vanilla essence (extract), if liked. Cover.

Quantity	Time on Full Power			
	600–650w	700–750w	800–850w	900–1000w
225 g/8 oz/ 1⅓ cups	12 mins	10½ mins	9 mins	8–9 mins

Standing time: 2 minutes.

Chill until ready to serve.

Gooseberries

Cooking: Wash, top and tail. Put in a thin layer in a shallow dish or casserole dish (Dutch oven). Sprinkle with sugar, to taste. Cover with clingfilm (plastic wrap), rolled back at one edge, or a lid.

Stir gently once or twice during cooking.

Quantity	Time on Full Power			
	600–650w	700–750w	800–850w	900–1000w
225 g/8 oz	4 mins	3½ mins	3 mins	2½–3 mins
450 g/1 lb	8 mins	7 mins	6 mins	5½–6 mins

Standing time: 2 minutes.

Grapefruit

Cooking: It is not possible to grill (broil) grapefruit in the microwave unless it has a browning element, but this method gives similar results. Halve the fruit, place in individual dishes and separate the segments with a serrated edged knife in the usual way. Sprinkle the halves with brown sugar and place in the microwave in a ring.

Quantity	Time on Full Power			
	600–650w	700–750w	800–850w	900–1000w
1 half	1½ mins	1–1½ mins	1 min	1 min
4 halves	5–6 mins	4–4½ mins	3½–4 mins	3½ mins

Standing time: 2 minutes.

Greengages

Cooking: Wash, halve and remove the stones (pits). Put in a thin layer in a shallow dish or casserole dish (Dutch oven). Sprinkle with sugar, to taste.

Stir gently once or twice during cooking to coat in the juice.

Quantity	Time on Full Power			
	600–650w	700–750w	800–850w	900–1000w
225 g/8 oz	2–3 mins	1½–2½ mins	1–2 mins	1–1½ mins
450 g/1 lb	4–5 mins	3½–4 mins	3–3½ mins	2½–3 mins

Standing time: 2 minutes.

Oranges, caramelised

Cooking: Make a caramel syrup (see page 42). Cut the rind and pith off four oranges. Slice and arrange in a shallow dish. Pour over the caramel.

Quantity	Time on Full Power			
	600–650w	700–750w	800–850w	900–1000w
4	1½ mins	1½ mins	1 min	1 min

Standing time: None.

Leave until completely cold, then chill before serving.

Peaches and nectarines

Cooking: Wash, halve or slice, removing the stones (pits), or leave whole. Put the fruit in a shallow dish or casserole dish (Dutch oven). Slices should be arranged in a thin layer; place halves cut sides down; arrange whole fruit round the edge of the dish. Sprinkle with a little sugar, to taste, or add a sugar syrup (see To poach fruit, page 147) and add a piece of cinnamon stick or the grated rind of a lemon or orange, if liked. Cover with clingfilm (plastic wrap), rolled back at one edge, or a lid.

Stir slices gently and rearrange the halves or whole fruit once during cooking. Slip the skins off after cooking, if liked.

Quantity	Time on Full Power			
	600–650w	700–750w	800–850w	900–1000w
2	2 mins	1½–2 mins	1½ mins	1–1½ mins
4	4 mins	3½ mins	3 mins	2½–3 mins

Standing time: 2 minutes.

Pears

Cooking: Wash, peel, halve and core, then quarter or slice, if liked, or leave whole. Put slices, halves or quarters in a thin layer in a shallow dish or casserole dish (Dutch oven). Arrange whole fruit round the edge of the dish. Sprinkle with sugar, to taste, or add a sugar syrup (see To poach fruit, page 147) and add a pinch of cinnamon, cloves, mixed (apple-pie) spice or the grated rind of a lemon or orange. Cover with clingfilm (plastic wrap), rolled back at one edge, or a lid.

Stir slices gently and rearrange halves or whole fruit once during cooking.

Quantity	Time on Full Power			
	600–650w	700–750w	800–850w	900–1000w
225 g/8 oz	4½–6 mins	4–5 mins	3–4 mins	2½–3 mins
450 g/1 lb	9–12 mins	8–10 mins	6–8 mins	5–6 mins

Standing time: 2 minutes.

Plums

Cooking: Wash, halve and remove the stones (pits).
Put in a thin layer in a shallow dish or casserole dish (Dutch oven).
Sprinkle with sugar, to taste.

Stir gently once or twice during cooking to coat in the juice.

Quantity	Time on Full Power			
	600–650w	700–750w	800–850w	900–1000w
225 g/8 oz	2–3 mins	1½–2½ mins	1–2 mins	1–1½ mins
450 g/1 lb	4–5 mins	3½–4 mins	3–3½ mins	2½–3 mins

Standing time: 2 minutes.

Raspberries

Cooking: Wash and remove any stalks. Put in a thin layer in a shallow dish or casserole dish (Dutch oven). Sprinkle with sugar, to taste. Add the grated rind of an orange, if liked. Cover with clingfilm (plastic wrap), rolled back at one edge, or a lid.

Stir gently once during cooking.

Quantity	Time on Full Power			
	600–650w	700–750w	800–850w	900–1000w
225 g/8 oz	2–2½ mins	1½–2 mins	1–1½ mins	1 min
450 g/1 lb	3–5 mins	2½–4 mins	2–3 mins	2 mins

Standing time: 2 minutes.

Redcurrants

Cooking: Wash the fruit and strip off the stalks
with the prongs of a fork. Put in a thin layer in a shallow dish or casserole
dish (Dutch oven). Sprinkle with sugar, to taste. Cover with clingfilm
(plastic wrap), rolled back at one edge, or a lid.

Stir or shake gently once or twice during cooking.

Quantity	Time on Full Power			
	600–650w	700–750w	800–850w	900–1000w
225 g/8 oz	2–2½ mins	1½–2 mins	1–1½ mins	1 min
450 g/1 lb	3–5 mins	2½–4 mins	2–3 mins	2 mins

Standing time: 2 minutes.

Rhubarb

Cooking: Wash, trim and cut into short lengths.
Put in a shallow dish or casserole dish (Dutch oven). Sprinkle generously
with sugar, to taste and add the grated rind of an orange, if liked, or a little
grated fresh root ginger. Cover with clingfilm (plastic wrap), rolled back at
one edge, or a lid.

Stir gently once or twice during cooking.

Quantity	Time on Full Power			
	600–650w	700–750w	800–850w	900–1000w
225 g/8 oz	4 mins	3½ mins	3 mins	2½–3 mins
450 g/1 lb	8 mins	7 mins	5½ mins	4½–5 mins

Standing time: 2 minutes.

Breads, Biscuits, Pastry and Cakes

Conventional baking uses a dry heat, which gives the traditional colour and texture to breads, biscuits (cookies), pastry (paste) and cakes. For this reason, these foods will not look the same when cooked in a microwave. This does not mean that the microwave is completely redundant when it comes to baking, however. Microwaved sponge cakes and puddings have a delicious light, soft texture and moist, sweet biscuits like flapjacks microwave quickly and extremely well. The various processes of yeast bread-making can be speeded up in the microwave and you can actually cook bread in the microwave too. The finished loaf will need browning and crisping conventionally, however, or, if you prefer, it can be coated with seeds, nuts or grains to make it look more appetising. Pastry doesn't crisp and brown, but you can cook a pastry case (pie shell) ready to be filled and although you can't cook conventional pies in the microwave, you can defrost them and some can be reheated (see Convenience foods, pages 34–5).

Microwave tips for breads and biscuits (cookies)

To warm soft rolls, brioches and croissants
Arrange in a circle on kitchen paper (paper towels) on a plate or in a basket. Cover with another sheet of kitchen paper. Microwave, checking very frequently, for 15–20 seconds per piece until warm. Do not allow to become hot or they will toughen as they cool.

To warm taco shells or soft flour tortillas
Arrange on a sheet of kitchen paper (paper towels) – shells in a circle, tortillas in a stack – with another sheet over the top. Heat on Full Power for 1–2 minutes until warm.

To refresh stale biscuits (cookies)

This works equally well for crisps (chips). Spread out on kitchen paper (paper towels) on a plate. Microwave on Full Power for 30 seconds to 1 minute until they feel warm. Leave to cool – they will crisp as they become cold. If still slightly soft, microwave for a few seconds more.

To refresh stale bread

Slice if the loaf is whole. Wrap in kitchen paper (paper towels) and microwave on Full Power for 10 seconds for six slices. Don't overcook or the bread will toughen.

To make dried breadcrumbs

Crumble bread in the usual way in a blender or food processor (including the crusts). Spread 100 g/4 oz/2 cups crumbs on a large plate and Microwave for 2½–4 minutes, stirring every minute until crisp. Leave until cold, then store in an airtight container.

To make toasted buttered crumbs

Melt a knob of butter or margarine in a bowl covered with a sheet of kitchen paper (paper towel) on Full Power for 10–20 seconds. Stir in the crumbs. Spread on a plate and microwave on Full Power for 1½–2½ minutes. Stir once or twice during cooking until crisp and golden. You can add flavourings such as garlic or onion granules, curry or chilli powder to the crumbs before cooking, if liked.

Croûtons

Croûtons are a delicious way to brighten up soups, salads, etc. and there is no quicker way to make them than in the microwave.

Cut the crusts off three slices of bread and cut the bread into small cubes. Place in a single layer on a plate. Microwave on Full Power for 3½–6 minutes, tossing every minute until crisp and dry.

General rules for bread

When using your microwave to make bread, it is worth remembering the following general rules.

- Wholemeal bread will have a better colour than white when cooked in the microwave.

- Bread crust will not brown or crisp so, after cooking, place the loaf under a hot grill (broiler) for a few minutes on each side to brown and crisp the crust. Alternatively, brush with a little beaten egg and sprinkle with toasted sesame seeds, poppy seeds, whole grains or rolled oats before cooking to enhance the appearance.

- If you prefer to cook your bread in the conventional way, you can use your microwave to warm the flour to speed up proving. Put the measured flour in a large bowl and cook on Full Power for about 2 minutes until warm through. Stir, then continue with your normal recipe.

- You can also prove the dough in the microwave. Put the kneaded dough in a large bowl, cover with a clean cloth or clingfilm (plastic wrap), rolled back at one edge, and cook on Full Power for 10–15 seconds. Leave to stand for 5 minutes. Repeat this process five or six times until the dough is doubled in bulk. Do not be tempted to give longer bursts or you will make the dough too hot and kill the yeast.

Defrosting bread

- Uncut loaves can be partially defrosted, then left to stand to finish the process. If you try to defrost it right through, you will toughen the outside.

- Cut loaves can be totally defrosted – microwave until they feel just soft when gently squeezed.

- You can also defrost individual slices, rolls, croissants, etc., wrapped in kitchen paper (paper towels). See individual entries.

- Rolls, buns, etc., can also be warmed from frozen in one action. Simply add on 5–10 seconds per item to the times given. You can do this in a basket lined with a napkin, ready for serving, if liked.

General rules for cakes

Sponge cakes

Small and large sponge cakes can be cooked with excellent results. Use your conventional recipes and follow these guidelines.

- To give colour to plain cakes, substitute 15 g/½ oz/2 tbsp custard powder for the same quantity of self-raising (self-rising) flour and add an extra 1.5 ml/¼ tsp baking powder to the mixture.
  or
  Use light brown sugar instead of caster (superfine).
  or
  Use wholemeal flour instead of white.

- To make chocolate cake, substitute cocoa (unsweetened chocolate) powder for the custard powder.

- For coffee cake, add 15 ml/1 tbsp instant coffee, dissolved in the milk.

- Make the mixture slightly wetter than when cooking conventionally (add an extra 15 ml/1 tbsp milk for every egg used).

- Don't grease the container if it is plastic. If pottery or Pyrex are used, grease it very lightly and line the base of the container with greaseproof (waxed) paper. Do not over-grease or flour the container or it will give an unpleasant crust to the cake.

- Take care not to overcook cakes 'baked' in the microwave or they will be unpleasantly dry. A microwaved sponge cake will rise considerably and should still have damp spots on the top when it is removed from the oven. These will dry out as it cools. The cake is cooked when it is risen and is beginning to shrink away from the sides of the container.

- Always stand the cake container on a microwave rack or an upturned small plate for cooking. This helps to distribute the microwaves more evenly.

- Never cover a cake when cooking.

- The cake will not be spoiled if you open the oven to check after the minimum cooking time. Unlike a conventionally baked cake, it will rise up again as soon as you continue to cook it.

- For small (fairy) cakes, make up a 1-egg quantity of sponge cake mixture. Arrange six or seven double-thickness paper cakes cases (cup cake papers) in a circle on a plate and place on an upturned small plate or microwave rack. Half-fill with the sponge mixture. Microwave on Full Power for 1½–3 minutes, turning and rearranging once after 1 minute. Cool on a wire rack.

Fruit cakes
- Make in your normal way but use dark brown sugar and a few drops of gravy browning for extra colour.

- Always make a hollow in the centre to ensure the cake cooks in the centre – or use a microwave ring container and have a ring-shaped cake!

- Wrap the cake in foil before standing to help the cooking process.

- Cook on Medium-Low. Check after 10 minutes, then at 1-minute intervals until beginning to shrink from the sides of the container. The cake should feel just firm to the touch and a cocktail stick (toothpick) inserted in the centre will come out clean.

- There may still be moist spots on the top when the cake is cooked.

- For Christmas cake, don't add alcohol to the mixture before cooking but when cold, pierce well on both sides with a skewer and pour 15–30 ml/1–2 tbsp brandy or rum over each side (or use orange juice if you prefer). Wrap in a double thickness of foil and store for at least 1 month to mature.

Scones (biscuits)

Plain, white scones can be cooked, using your normal recipe, on a browning dish (see pages 22–3) to give a better colour and crisper crust. Alternatively, use self-raising (self-rising) wholemeal flour, or half wholemeal and half white. If sweetening, use brown instead of white sugar. You can also make cheese and fruit scones.

Biscuits (cookies)

Crisp biscuit recipes don't work well in a microwave, but it is ideal for making sticky bars, such as flapjacks, and crumbly ones like shortbread, that are cooked in a slab, then cut into fingers. You can melt the fat and syrup for flapjacks in a mixing bowl on Full Power for 1–2 minutes and then stir in the remaining ingredients. You can also soften the butter and sugar in the microwave on Low for 30 seconds before creaming for shortbread.

Biscuit base
Melt the butter or margarine in a fairly large bowl, covered with a sheet of kitchen paper (paper towel), on Full Power for 1 minute. Stir in the biscuit crumbs, then press into the sides and base of a flan dish (pie pan). Cook on Full Power for 2 minutes and leave to cool, then chill before filling.

Pastry (paste)

Pastry will not brown or crisp in the microwave. You can, however, defrost it in the microwave and cook a pastry case (pie shell) (see page 178).

Cooked pastry dishes
Reheat from frozen (see Convenience foods, pages 34–5). A 20 cm/8 in flan (pie) quiche or tart will take about 4 minutes on Medium-Low. Leave to stand for 5 minutes, then microwave on Full Power for 3–4 minutes until piping hot. The pastry should feel just warm, but the filling will be hotter. Test by inserting a knife down through the centre. Leave for 5 seconds, then remove. It should feel piping hot to the touch. If not, cook for a minute or two longer.

Pizza

To reheat ready-cooked pizzas, see Convenience Foods, page 36.

Defrosting and cooking times for bread, biscuits, pastry and cakes

Note that many of these times are in seconds, not minutes.

Bagels

Defrosting: Place on kitchen paper (paper towels) and cover with another sheet of kitchen paper.

Turn over once halfway through defrosting.

Quantity	Time on Medium-Low (all power outputs)
1	30 secs
2	1 min
4	2 mins

Standing time: 1–2 bagels: 2 minutes.
4 bagels: 3 minutes.

Cooking: Bagels cannot be cooked in the microwave.

Warming: Place on kitchen paper and cover with another sheet of kitchen paper.

Check every few seconds and don't allow them to overheat or they will become tough or hard.

Quantity	Time on Full Power (all power outputs)
1	10–15 secs
2	20–30 secs
4	40–50 secs

Standing time: None.

Bread

Defrosting: If defrosting a whole loaf, leave in its wrapper but open the end. If defrosting individual slices, wrap in kitchen paper (paper towels). The time is the same for all power outputs.

Turn over halfway through defrosting. Check individual slices before the end as they may defrost more quickly than you expect.

For high power outputs, you may get better results by defrosting on Low, and increasing the standing time.

Quantity	Time on Medium-Low (all power outputs)
1 medium slice	20–30 secs
Small uncut loaf (any type)	4–5 mins
Large uncut loaf (any type)	7–8 mins
Small sliced loaf (any type)	3–4 mins
Large sliced loaf (any type)	6–7 mins

Standing time: 1 slice: None.
Small loaves (cut or uncut): 5–10 minutes.
Large loaves (cut or uncut): 10–15 minutes.

Cooking: Make your bread dough in the normal way.
Leave to prove, or prove in the microwave. Cover with clingfilm (plastic wrap) or kitchen paper.

Microwave on Full Power for 10–15 seconds only.
Leave to stand for 5 minutes.

Repeat this process five or six times until the dough is doubled in bulk. Knock back (punch down), shape, place in a loaf container or other suitable container and prove as before. Glaze with beaten egg and sprinkle with seeds (see page 25).

Cook until spongy, risen and shrinking slightly from the edge of the container.

Quantity	Time on Full Power			
	600–650w	700–750w	800–850w	900–1000w
450 g/1 lb loaf	6 mins	5–5½ mins	4½–5 mins	4½ mins

Standing time: 5–10 minutes.

Turn out on to a wire rack to cool.

Bread rolls

Defrosting: Place on kitchen paper (paper towels) and cover with another sheet of kitchen paper.

Turn over once halfway through defrosting.

Quantity	Time on Medium-Low (all power outputs)
1	30 secs
2	1 min
4	2 mins

Standing time: 1–2 rolls: 2 minutes.
4 rolls: 3 minutes.

Cooking: Make your bread dough in the normal way.
Leave to prove, or prove in the microwave. Cover with clingfilm (plastic wrap) or kitchen paper.

Microwave on Full Power for 10–15 seconds only.
Leave to stand for 5 minutes.

Repeat this process five or six times until the dough is doubled in bulk. Knock back (punch down), shape, place well apart on a plate. Cover and prove as before. Glaze with beaten egg and sprinkle with seeds (see page 25). Cook according to the table overleaf until spongy and risen.

Quantity	Time on Full Power			
	600–650w	700–750w	800–850w	900–1000w
6–8 rolls (450 g/1 lb dough)	6 mins	5–5½ mins	4½–5 mins	4½ mins

Standing time: 5 minutes.
Transfer to a wire rack to cool.

Warming: Place on kitchen paper (paper towels)
and cover with another sheet of kitchen paper.

Check every few seconds and don't overheat or they will
become tough or hard.

Quantity	Time on Full Power (all power outputs)
1	10–15 secs
2	20–30 secs
4	40–50 secs

Standing time: None.

Currant or mixed fruit buns

Defrosting: Place on kitchen paper (paper towels)
and cover with another sheet of kitchen paper.

Turn over once halfway through defrosting.

Quantity	Time on Medium-Low (all power outputs)
1	30 secs
2	1 min
4	2 mins

Standing time: 1–2 buns: 4 minutes.
4 buns: 6 minutes.

Cooking: Make your bread dough in the normal way. Leave to prove, or
prove in the microwave. Cover with clingfilm (plastic wrap) or kitchen
paper (paper towels).

Microwave on Full Power for 10–15 seconds only.
Leave to stand for 5 minutes.

Repeat this process five or six times until the dough is doubled in bulk.
Knock back (punch down), shape and place well apart on a plate.
Cover and prove as before. Glaze with beaten egg and sprinkle with
light brown or demerara sugar. Cook according to the times
in the table opposite until spongy and risen.

Quantity	Time on Full Power			
	600–650w	700–750w	800–850w	900–1000w
6–8 buns (450 g/1 lb dough)	6 mins	5–5½ mins	4½–5 mins	4½ mins

Standing time: 5 minutes.
Transfer to a wire rack to cool.

Warming: Place on kitchen paper and cover with another sheet of kitchen paper.

Check every few seconds and don't overheat or they will become tough or hard.

Quantity	Time on Full Power (all power outputs)
1	10–15 secs
2	20–30 secs
4	40–50 secs

Standing time: None.

Dumplings

These can be dropped around the top of a casserole for the last 5–8 minutes' cooking time or can be cooked separately.

Cooking: Place in a circle on a sheet of greaseproof (waxed) paper.

Cook until fluffy and set.

Quantity	Time on Full Power			
	600–650w	700–750w	800–850w	900–1000w
6	6 mins	5 mins	4 mins	3½–4 mins

Standing time: 1 minute.

Brioches

Defrosting: Place on kitchen paper (paper towels) and cover with another sheet of kitchen paper.

Turn over once halfway through defrosting.

Quantity	Time on Medium-Low (all power outputs)
1	30 secs
2	1 min
4	2 mins

Standing time: 1–2 brioches: 2 minutes.
4 brioches: 3 minutes.

Cooking: Make your dough in the normal way.
Leave to prove, or prove in the microwave. Cover with clingfilm (plastic wrap) or kitchen paper.

Microwave on Full Power for 10–15 seconds only. Leave to stand for 5 minutes. Repeat this process five or six times until the dough is doubled in bulk.

Knock back (punch down), shape, place in double-thickness paper cake cases (cup cake papers), well apart on a plate. Cover and prove as before. Glaze with beaten egg. Cook according to the times in the table below until spongy and risen.

Quantity	Time on Full Power			
	600–650w	700–750w	800–850w	900–1000w
6–8 brioches (450 g/1 lb dough)	6 mins	5–5½ mins	4½–5 mins	4½ mins

Standing time: 5 minutes.
Transfer to a wire rack to cool.

Warming: Place on kitchen paper and cover with another sheet of kitchen paper.

Check every few seconds and don't overheat or they will become tough or hard.

Quantity	Time on Full Power (all power outputs)
1	10–15 secs
2	20–30 secs
4	40–50 secs

Standing time: None.

Chapattis

Defrosting: Place on kitchen paper (paper towels) and cover with another sheet of kitchen paper.

Turn over halfway through defrosting.

Quantity	Time on Medium-Low (all power outputs)
1	30 secs
2	1 min
4	2 mins

Standing time: 1–2 chapattis: 2 minutes.
4 chapattis: 3 minutes.

Cooking: For best results, cook home-made chapattis conventionally.

Warming: Place on kitchen paper and cover with another sheet of kitchen paper.

Check every few seconds and don't overheat or they will become tough or hard.

Quantity	Time on Full Power (all power outputs)
1	10–15 secs
2	20–30 secs
4	40–50 secs

Standing time: None.

Croissants

Defrosting: Place on kitchen paper (paper towels) and cover with another sheet of kitchen paper.

Turn over once halfway through defrosting.

Quantity	Time on Medium-Low (all power outputs)
1	30 secs
2	1 min
4	2 mins

Standing time: 1–2 croissants: 2 minutes.
4 croissants: 3 minutes.

Cooking: Home-made croissants are not suitable for cooking in the microwave.

Warming: Place on kitchen paper and cover with another sheet of kitchen paper.

Check every few seconds and don't overheat or they will become tough or hard.

Quantity	Time on Full Power (all power outputs)
1	10–15 secs
2	20–30 secs
4	40–50 secs

Standing time: None.

Doughnuts

Defrosting: Place on kitchen paper (paper towels) and cover with another sheet of kitchen paper.

Turn over once halfway through defrosting.

Quantity	Time on Medium-Low (all power outputs)
1	45 secs
2	1½ mins
4	2½ mins

Standing time: 1–2 doughnuts: 2 minutes.
4 doughnuts: 3 minutes.

Cooking: Only special microwave-and-serve doughnuts are suitable for cooking in the microwave. Follow the instructions on the packet.

Warming/refreshing: Place on kitchen paper and cover with another sheet of kitchen paper.

Check every few seconds and don't overheat or they will become tough or hard and be warned, if filled with jam (conservo), it will get very hot.

Quantity	Time on Medium (all power outputs)
1	20 secs
2	30–40 secs
4	1 min

Standing time: None.

Cream doughnuts

Defrosting: Place on kitchen paper (paper towels) and cover with another sheet of kitchen paper.

Turn over once halfway through defrosting. Watch carefully to check the cream does not start to melt. If so, remove from the microwave immediately.

Quantity	Time on Medium-Low (all power outputs)
1	20–25 secs
2	40–50 secs
4	1½ mins

Standing time: 5 minutes.
Place in the fridge for a short while to chill the cream, if liked.

Naan breads

Defrosting: Place on kitchen paper (paper towels)
and cover with another sheet of kitchen paper.

Turn over halfway through defrosting.

Quantity	Time on Medium-Low (all power outputs)
1 large or 2 small	45 secs–1 min
2 large or 4 small	1½–2 mins

Standing time: 1 large or 2 small: 2 minutes.
2 large or 4 small: 3 minutes.

Cooking: For best results, cook home-made
naan breads conventionally.

Warming: Place on kitchen paper and cover with
another sheet of kitchen paper.

Check every few seconds and don't overheat or they will
become tough or hard.

Quantity	Time on Full Power (all power outputs)
1 large or 2 small	20–30 secs
2 large or 4 small	40 secs–1 min

Standing time: None.

Pitta breads

Defrosting: Place on kitchen paper (paper towels)
and cover with another sheet of kitchen paper.

Turn over halfway through defrosting.

Quantity	Time on Medium-Low (all power outputs)
1	30 secs
2	1 min
4	2 mins

Standing time: 1–2 pittas: 2 minutes.
4 pittas: 3 minutes.

Cooking: For best results, cook home-made pittas conventionally.

Warming: Place on kitchen paper and cover with another sheet of kitchen paper.

Check every few seconds and don't overheat or they will become tough or hard.

Quantity	Time on Full Power (all power outputs)
1	10–15 secs
2	20–30 secs
4	40–50 secs

Standing time: None.

Flour tortillas

Defrosting: Place a stack on kitchen paper (paper towels) and cover with another sheet of kitchen paper.

Peel off the tortillas as they defrost, and remove. Turn over the stack halfway through defrosting.

Quantity	Time on Medium-Low (all power outputs)
8	2 mins

Standing time: Wrap in foil and leave to stand while the remainder defrost.

Cooking: For best results, home-made tortillas
should be cooked in a frying pan (skillet).

Warming: Place a stack on kitchen paper and cover with
another sheet of kitchen paper.

Turn over halfway through warming.

Quantity	Time on Full Power (all power outputs)
8	45 secs–1 min

Standing time: None.

Sponge cakes

Defrosting: Defrost in the wrapper or
unwrap and place on kitchen paper (paper towels).

If your cake is cream-filled, check frequently. If there are signs
of the cream melting, stop immediately.

Quantity	Time on Medium-Low (all power outputs)
1 × 15 cm/6 in cake	3–5 mins
1 × 20 cm/8 in cake	5–8 mins

Standing time: Up to 2 hours.

Cooking: Prepare a 2-egg or 3-egg mixture
(see guidelines, page 160). Turn into an 18 cm/7 in or 20 cm/8 in
microwave cake container or very lightly greased deep, round dish,
base-lined with non-stick baking parchment. Stand the dish on a
microwave rack or upturned small plate.

Cook until beginning to shrink from the sides but still
with a few moist spots on top.

Quantity	Time on Full Power			
	600–650w	700–750w	800–850w	900–1000w
1 × 18 cm/7 in cake	6 mins	5 mins	4 mins	3½–4 mins
1 × 20 cm/8 in cake	7–8 mins	6–7 mins	5–6 mins	4½–5 mins

Standing time: 10 minutes.

Turn out on to a wire rack. When completely cold, split and fill as required.

Sponge pudding

Defrosting: Leave in its basin or wrapper.

Quantity	Time on Medium-Low (all power outputs)
1 × 15 cm/6 in pudding	4–6 mins
1 × 20 cm/8 in pudding	5–8 mins

Standing time: 10 minutes or until completely defrosted.

Cooking: Prepare a 2-egg or 3-egg mixture (see guidelines, page 160). Put jam (conserve) or golden (light corn) syrup, according to your recipe, in the base of a 15 cm/6 in or 20 cm/8 in pudding basin, base-lined with a circle of non-stick baking parchment. Stand the dish on a microwave rack or upturned small plate.

Cook until beginning to shrink from the sides but still with a few moist spots on top.

Quantity	Time on Full Power			
	600–650w	700–750w	800–850w	900–1000w
1 × 18 cm/7 in pudding	6 mins	5 mins	4 mins	3½–4 mins
1 × 20 cm/8 in pudding	7–8 mins	6–7 mins	5–6 mins	4½–5 mins

Standing time: 5 minutes.

Turn out before serving.

Reheating: A whole pudding may be reheated in its basin. Individual slices should be placed in a small bowl.

Quantity	Time on Medium			
	600–650w	700–750w	800–850w	900–1000w
1 × 18 cm/7 in pudding	6 mins	5 mins	4 mins	3½–4 mins
1 × 20 cm/8 in pudding	8 mins	7 mins	5 mins	3½ mins
1 slice	1–1½ mins	1 min	45 secs–1 min	45 secs

Standing time: 2 minutes.

Fruit cake

Defrosting: Defrost in its wrapper or unwrap and place on kitchen paper (paper towels).

Turn over once halfway through defrosting. Stop if it is getting warm.

Quantity	Time on Medium-Low (all power outputs)
1 × 15 cm/6 in cake	5 mins
1 × 20 cm/8 in cake	8 mins

Standing time: Up to 2 hours, until completely defrosted.

Cooking: Prepare the mixture in your usual way, checking the guidelines on page 161. Turn into a suitable-sized microwave cake container or very lightly greased deep, round dish, base-lined with non-stick baking parchment. Make a slight hollow in the centre. Stand the dish on a microwave rack or upturned small plate.

Cook for the time given, then give 1-minute bursts until the cake is beginning to shrink from the sides but still has a few moist spots on top.

Note: The time given in the table opposite is the initial cooking time. There will be several 1-minute bursts after this.

Quantity	Time on Medium-Low			
	600–650w	700–750w	800–850w	900–1000w
1 × 20 cm/ 8 in cake	12 mins	11 mins	10 mins	9 mins

Standing time: 10 minutes.

Turn out on to a wire rack to cool completely.

Scones (biscuits)

Defrosting: Arrange on kitchen paper (paper towels)
and cover with another sheet of kitchen paper.

Turn over halfway through thawing.

Quantity	Time on Medium-Low (all power outputs)
1	30 secs
2	1 min
4	2 mins
8	4 mins

Standing time: 1–4 scones: 2 minutes.
8 scones: 3 minutes.

Cooking: Prepare the mixture in your usual way, checking the guidelines
on page 162. Cut into rounds using a 5 cm/2 in biscuit (cookie) cutter.
Place eight in a circle on a piece of greaseproof (waxed) paper on a plate.
Brush with melted butter and sprinkle with demerara sugar for sweet
scones, toasted sesame or poppy seeds for savoury ones.

Turn over halfway through cooking. Cook until risen and spongy.

Quantity	Time on Full Power			
	600–650w	700–750w	800–850w	900–1000w
8	4 mins	3 mins	2 mins	1¾–2 mins

Standing time: 2 minutes.

Transfer to a wire rack to cool or serve warm.

Pastry (paste)

Defrosting: Use this method for defrosting frozen block puff pastry or shortcrust (basic pie crust). Leave in its wrapper or unwrap and place on kitchen paper (paper towels) if more convenient.

Turn over once during defrosting time. Do not increase microwaving time or it will start to cook around the edges.

Quantity	Time on Medium-Low (all power outputs)
225–350 g/ 8–12 oz	2–3 mins

Standing time: Up to 1 hour, wrapped in foil, shiny side in. Leave until completely defrosted.

Cooking: This is suitable only for a pastry case (pie shell) prior to filling. To make an 18 cm/7 in case, roll out 175 g/6 oz shortcrust pastry. Use to line a flan dish (pie pan). Prick the base with a fork and line with a double thickness of kitchen paper.

Quantity	Time on Full Power			
	600–650w	700–750w	800–850w	900–1000w
1 × 18 cm/7 in case	5 mins	4 mins	3 mins	2½–3 mins

Standing time: 2 minutes.

Quiche

For frozen quiches, see Convenience foods, page 34.

Cooking: Make a pastry case (pie shell) as above. Add the filling in your usual way and sprinkle with cheese.

Quantity	Time on Medium			
	600–650w	700–750w	800–850w	900–1000w
1 × 18 cm/7 in case	18–20 mins	17 mins	15 mins	12–15 mins

Standing time: 5 minutes, until completely set.

Place under a hot grill (broiler) to brown the top, if liked.

Cheesecake

Defrosting: Remove any foil container.
Place on kitchen paper (paper towels).

Do not try to microwave for longer than the time given or it will melt.

Quantity	Time on Medium-Low (all power outputs)
1 × 15–17 cm/ 6–7 in cake	3 mins

Standing time: 25–30 minutes, or until completely defrosted.

Cooking: Home-made cheesecakes are not suitable for cooking in the microwave.

Eclairs and profiteroles

Defrosting: Arrange on kitchen paper (paper towels).

Check during defrosting for signs of the chocolate or cream melting. If it does, stop immediately.

Quantity	Time on Medium-Low (all power outputs)
2 éclairs or 4 profiteroles	15–20 secs
4 éclairs or 8 profiteroles	30–45 secs

Standing time: 10 minutes, or until completely defrosted.

Cooking: Home-made éclairs and profiteroles are not suitable for cooking in the microwave.

Flapjacks

Defrosting: Flapjacks keep well in an airtight tin,
so there is no need to freeze or defrost them.

Cooking: Press the mixture into a lightly greased, shallow, square or
round dish. Place on a microwave rack.

Quantity	Time on Full Power			
	600–650w	700–750w	800–850w	900–1000w
1 × 20 cm/8 in dish	6 mins	5 mins	4½ mins	4 mins

Standing time: 5 minutes.

Cut into fingers, then leave to cool.

Shortbread

Defrosting: Shortbread will keep in an airtight container for a week or
two so you are unlikely to need to freeze or defrost it.

Cooking: Press your usual mixture into a lightly greased 18 cm/7 in
square or round, shallow container. Prick all over with a fork.

Cook until just firm.

Quantity	Time on Full Power			
	600–650w	700–750w	800–850w	900–1000w
1 × 18 cm/7 in dish	6 mins	5 mins	4 mins	3½–4 mins

Standing time: 5 minutes.

Mark into pieces, then dust with caster (superfine) sugar
and leave to cool.

Drinks, Preserves and Sundries

s I have already said, your microwave is a most versatile tool. This chapter includes all kinds of ideas for getting the very best out of every facility it has to offer.

Drinks

Your microwave is perfect for making and reheating single drinks of all kinds. A word of warning, however – when heating a mug of liquid to drink, make sure the container is microwave-safe or it will become hot and could burn your lips. Always stir it before drinking to distribute the heat evenly.

To reheat drinks
Place in a mug or cup and microwave on Full Power for 1–2 minutes, then stir before serving.

Coffee, ground

Heating: Put 10 ml/2 tsp ground coffee per person in a jug.
Pour in a suitable amount of cold water.

Stir once halfway through heating. Stop when the coffee froths but is not quite boiling.

Quantity	Time on Full Power			
	600–650w	700–750w	800–850w	900–1000w
1 cup	1½ mins	1¼ mins	1 min	1 min

Standing time: 2 minutes.

Draw a cold spoon across the surface to settle the grounds.
Pour as usual.

Coffee, instant

Heating: Pour cold water or milk or half milk and half water into a cup or mug.

Heat until just boiling.

Quantity	Time on Full Power			
	600–650w	700–750w	800–850w	900–1000w
1 cup	1½ mins	1¼ mins	1 min	1 min

Standing time: None.

Stir in coffee granules or powder and add a dash of cold milk, if liked.

Drinking chocolate

Heating: Fill a mug with cold milk, leaving a 2.5 cm/1 in headspace.

Quantity	Time on Full Power			
	600–650w	700–750w	800–850w	900–1000w
1 mug	2 mins	1½ mins	1¼ mins	1–1¼ mins

Standing time: None.

Add drinking (sweetened) chocolate powder, to taste.
Whisk with a fork or small wire whisk until blended and frothy.

Milk

Heating: Pour into a cup or measuring jug.

Quantity	Time on Full Power			
	600–650w	700–750w	800–850w	900–1000w
200 ml/7 fl oz/ scant 1 cup	2 mins	1½ mins	1¼ mins	1–1¼ mins

Standing time: None.

Stir before use on cereals or in hot drinks.

Honey and lemon drink

This is very soothing when you have a cold or sore throat.

Heating: Put 30 ml/2 tbsp clear honey in a mug with the juice of 1 small lemon. Top up with water.

Quantity	Time on Full Power			
	600–650w	700–750w	800–850w	900–1000w
1 mug	2 mins	1½ mins	1 min	1 min

Standing time: None.
Stir well and sip. Stir in a little more honey, if liked.

Tea

If you don't want to put the kettle on, make yourself a hot cuppa in the microwave!

Heating: Put a teabag in a mug and top up with cold water.

Quantity	Time on Full Power			
	600–650w	700–750w	800–850w	900–1000w
1 mug	2 mins	1½ mins	1 min	1 min

Standing time: 1 minute.

Stir, remove the bag and add milk or a slice of lemon, to taste.

Mulled wine

Makes 6 glasses.

Heating: Pour a bottle of red wine in a large bowl. Stir in 30 ml/2 tbsp caster (superfine) sugar, 30 ml/2 tbsp brandy, a few slices of orange and lemon, 5 cm/2 in piece of cinnamon stick and 2 cloves.

Stir twice. Do not allow to boil.

Quantity	Time on Medium			
	600–650w	700–750w	800–850w	900–1000w
1 bottle	5 mins	4 mins	3 mins	2½–3 mins

Standing time: 1 minute.

Preserves

Making jam (conserve) and other preserves in the microwave is clean and efficient. You can use your normal recipes. Follow these general rules for best results.

- Do not make more than 1.75 kg/4 lb jam in one go and no more than 450 g/1 lb lemon curd, or other flavoured curd.

- Use your microwave to sterilise the jars. Pour 150 ml/¼ pt/⅔ cup water in each clean jar (make sure there are no metal bands). Microwave on Full Power until the water is boiling, then microwave for a further 1 minute. Remove from the oven using oven gloves. Pour out the water, then drain upside down on kitchen paper (paper towels).

  Note: This method should not be used to sterilise baby bottles, bowls, etc.

- Use your microwave to warm the preserving sugar before use – 450 g/1 lb will take 2–3 minutes on Medium.

- Choose a very large bowl to prevent boiling over – it should have at least three times the capacity of the ingredients. So for 900 g/2 lb fruit, use a bowl about 3.25 litres/6 pt/15 cups.

- Dissolve the warmed sugar completely in the fruit before starting to boil the mixture to setting point.

- Stir and test for a set after every minute. Do not use a conventional sugar thermometer: instead test by the 'wrinkle' test. Put a small spoonful of the mixture on a cold saucer. Push your finger through the jam. If the surface wrinkles, setting point has been reached.

- Use oven gloves to remove the bowl from the oven – it will be very hot.

- Pot, cover and label in your usual way.

Chutney
Use your normal chutney recipe. Sterilise the jars (see general rules, above). Put the prepared ingredients in a large bowl. Cook on Full Power for 30 minutes. Stir well. Continue to cook in 5-minute bursts until thick and pulpy. Pot, cover and label. For safety precautions, see above.

Citrus curds

Sterilise the jar (see general rules, left). Use your normal recipe but make only 450 g/1 lb at a time. Put the fruit rind and juice, the sugar and butter in a large bowl.

Microwave on Full Power for 2–3 minutes until hot. Stir, then whisk in the eggs. Whisk every 30 seconds, until thick and smooth (see table below). Do not allow to boil. If it seems to be getting too hot before it thickens, reduce the power to Medium and continue in the same way.

Quantity	Time on Full Power			
	600–650w	700–750w	800–850w	900–1000w
450 g/1 lb	6 mins	5 mins	4 mins	3½–4 mins

Standing time: None.

Pot, label and store in your usual way.

Sundries and shortcuts

There are many simple tasks that your microwave can carry out, saving you time, effort and washing up. It is particularly useful for preparing individual ingredients in a recipe. Some of its uses, however, are a little more unusual – I have, in my time, dyed T-shirts and made play-dough in my microwave oven. Here is a selection of the best, from the mundane to the downright weird.

Note: Although your microwave is very good at drying small food items, don't try to dry wet clothes or papers in it. They might ignite!

To soften hardened brown sugar

Turn the block into a bowl and add a slice of bread. Cover with a plate and microwave on Full Power for 30 seconds. Leave to stand for 1 minute, then discard the bread and break up the block.

To puff up poppadoms

Put the poppadoms one at a time in the microwave and cook on Full Power for 45 seconds to 1 minute until puffed up. Turn over after 30 seconds.

To re-crisp breakfast cereal
Spread 1 portion on kitchen paper (paper towels) on a plate. Microwave on Full Power for 30–45 seconds, stirring halfway through heating. If necessary, heat a little longer until the cereal feels crisp. For larger quantities, heat in 30-second bursts until crisp. Leave until cold, then store in an airtight container.

To heat baby food (commercial jars)
Remove the metal cap and cover the jar with kitchen paper (paper towels). Heat on Full Power for 20–30 seconds. Stir well, and check the food is not too hot before serving.

Note: If you reheat homecooked baby food in the microwave, you must make it piping hot and then let it cool down. Never just warm it or you could cause food poisoning. Always check the temperature before giving it to your baby.

To heat baby milk (bottled formula)
Put the bottle of milk, with the teat cover on, in the microwave and heat on Full Power for 30–40 seconds. Shake thoroughly and test the temperature before feeding.

To dissolve gelatine
Put the measured amount of powdered gelatine in a small bowl with 45–60 ml/3–4 tbsp liquid from the recipe. Leave to soften for 5 minutes. Place the bowl in the microwave and microwave on Full Power for 30 seconds. Stir, then cook in 10-second bursts for up to 1 minute until completely dissolved. Do not allow to boil. Use immediately.

To make jelly (jello)
Break up the tablet and place the cubes in a measuring jug. Make up to 300 ml/½ pt/1¼ cups with water. Microwave on Full Power for 1½–2½ minutes. Stir until dissolved. Stir in ice cubes or cold water to make up to 600 ml/1 pt/2½ cups, then pour into a serving dish or mould. Leave until cold, then chill until set. Turn out if necessary and serve.

To loosen set jelly (jello)

This method may only be used for a jelly in a glass or plastic mould, **not** metal.

Place the mould in the microwave and microwave on Medium for 10–20 seconds. Gently pull the jelly from the sides of the mould, then invert on a plate, shake firmly and remove the mould.

To bring red wine to room temperature

Pour the bottle of wine into a large jug or glass carafe. Microwave on Full Power for 10–15 seconds. Leave to stand for 5 minutes, then either pour back into the bottle or serve from the jug.

To melt chocolate

Break up 100 g/4 oz/1 cup chocolate and place in a small bowl. Microwave on Full Power for 1½–3 minutes, stirring every 30 seconds until just shiny. Stir well to melt any remaining small pieces. Don't continue to heat once melted or it will burn.

To soften honey or golden (light corn) syrup

This method can be used to revive honey and syrup that have crystallised.

If in a jar, remove the lid. If in a can, spoon into a bowl or jug. Microwave on Full Power. 100 g/4 oz/⅓ cup will take 20–30 seconds but add on extra 10-second bursts, if necessary. Stir well and leave until cool before use.

To dry flowers

Arrange petals in a single layer on a piece of kitchen paper (paper towels) placed on a plate or directly on the turntable or floor of the oven. Microwave on Full Power for 1 minute. Turn the petals over and cook for a further 1 minute or until dry. Tip into a bowl and add a few drops of pot pourri oil for added fragrance.

To dry herbs

Herbs can be dried very quickly in the microwave. Wash fresh sprigs and then dry them on kitchen paper (paper towels). Do not remove the stalks – leave the sprigs whole. Chives, however, should be snipped into small pieces. Lay the herbs in a single layer on a sheet of kitchen paper on a large plate or on the turntable. Put a small cup of water beside the herbs to absorb some of the energy. Microwave on Full Power until the herbs lose their bright colour and will crumble easily. Check every 30 seconds and rearrange the sprigs every minute. Leave until cold, then crumble into an airtight container, discarding the stalks. Store in a cool, dark place.

To dye fabrics

Although you cannot dry clothes in the microwave, you can colour them. Synthetic fabrics won't work, however. Clothes with metal zips or fasteners cannot be dyed in the microwave. For best results, follow these guidelines.

- Dye only 225 g/8 oz of cotton or linen at one time.
- Wearing rubber gloves, empty a 100 g/4 oz container of Dylon Natural Dye into a large bowl.
- Stir in 200 ml/7 fl oz/scant 1 cup cold water, using a plastic or wooden stirrer, until the dye is completely dissolved.
- Blend in a further 400 ml/14 fl oz/1¾ cups cold water. Add the fabric and push down well until completely soaked and submerged.
- Put the bowl in a large roaster bag and tie with string.
- Microwave on Full Power for 3½–5 minutes.
- Remove from the cooker. Carefully open the bag and pour away the liquid.
- Rinse the fabric in cold water until the water is clear.
- Wash in warm suds, then dry away from direct heat.

To tie-dye: Knot the fabric in several places, tying it with string, elastic bands or knotting it with itself before immersing in the dye. Rinse, then untie.

Index